Easy Instructions
for Using Lotus

By

Walter W. Bell

Published by

Simple Software, Inc.

Simple Software, Inc.
2955 Hartley Rd.
Suite 102
Jacksonville, FL 32257
Ph (904)262-1442
Fax (904)268-8208

FIRST EDITION
1st Printing - January 1993

ISBN 1-880071-04-5

Manufactured in the United States of America

DEDICATION

This book is dedicated to all the people who want to know how to do things with their computer but do not have the time nor want to spend the effort finding out how.

The students I talk with don't want to dig into a book 600 pages long with lots of reading material to find out how to do a command like add a column. They just want the facts. "How do I do this? What keys do I press?" This book is for them.

It is also dedicated to the thousands of students I have had over the years that have helped me develop the approach in teaching step-by-step instructions.

Special thanks to

Allison Baker
Associate Editor

DISCLAIMER

No patent liability is assumed with respect to the use of the information contained herein. While every precaution has been taken in the preparation of this book, the publisher and author assume no responsibility for errors or omissions. Neither is any liability assumed for damages resulting from the use of the information contained herein. No liability is assumed by any of this books dealers or distributors for any loss or damage whether direct or indirect resulting from the use of information in this book.

Subjects Covered

1-Getting started 17
2-The Worksheet 31
3-Working with Words 61
4-Formulas 67
5-Formatting 77
6-Printing 95
7-Working with Files 121
8-Graphs 129
9-WYSIWYG 147
10-Working with a Database 151
11-Macros 163
12-Linking spreadsheets 177
13-Creating ASCII 181
14-Icons 185
15-Add ins 213
16-Index 220

TABLE OF CONTENTS

These are all of the shortcut instructions. We suggest you use the index in the back of the book to more easily find the commands you are looking for.

How to add graph to spreadsheet (embed it) 141
How to add titles to axes 131
How to add two cells together 70
How to advance the printer one line 101
How to align cell contents 62
How to align text across cells 64
How to assign page number to start with 117
How to attach add-ins 213
How to attach an explanation to a number 32
How to attach WYSIWYG 147
How to average column 71
How to avoid dangers 47
How to brighten the display 57
How to cancel menu or command 41
How to center words 62
How to center words across cells 64
How to change all column widths 81
How to change cell-pointer 57
How to change column width 59, 80
How to change directories 122
How to change display to bright 57
How to change font cartridge 119
How to change font in WYSIWYG 63
How to change font set 63
How to change format 78

How to change frame appearance 56
How to change graph axes 132
How to change margins 95, 110
How to change named print area 103
How to change paper size 110
How to change print default settings 95
How to change printer bin 119
How to change size of print 98
How to choose graph type 138
How to clear borders 102,113
How to clear footer 111
How to clear header 112
How to clear page break 60
How to clear print options 99
How to clear screen 25
How to clear the screen 25
How to clear the text attribute 65
How to close a window 83
How to combine worksheet data 125
How to compose characters 183
How to compress the whole printed spreadsheet 115
How to convert relative to absolute cell 49
How to copy balances forward 125
How to copy down 37
How to copy formulas or text from another file 125
How to copy more than one cell 36
How to copy one cell 35
How to copy range 36
How to copy to another spreadsheet 125
How to copy values from another file 125
How to copy WYSIWYG formats 148
How to correct mistakes 18,72
How to count entries 71

Table of Contents

How to create 3-Dimensional graph 138
How to create 7 good macros 167
How to create absolute expressions 48
How to create and/or formulas 74
How to create ASCII characters 181
How to create auto-executing macro 165
How to create auto-loading add-in 213
How to create auto-loading worksheet 166
How to create custom menu 173
How to create custom page size 110
How to create database query 154
How to create directory 122
How to create footer 97, 111
How to create graph 129
How to create graph grid 134
How to create graph group 136
How to create graph legends 130
How to create graph titles 130
How to create header 96, 111
How to create If conditions 72
How to create labels 61
How to create left border 113
How to create legends 130
How to create Lookups 75
How to create macro 163
How to create named-style 93
How to create quick graph 137
How to create relative expressions 48
How to create sample macros 167
How to create sequence of numbers 50, 152
How to create shadow box 90
How to create simple formulas 70
How to create table of files in sheet 124

How to create table of named print areas 104
How to create text file 109
How to create top border 112
How to data query 154
How to define learn range 164, 165
How to delete cells 33
How to delete columns 40
How to delete data automatically 160
How to delete file 123
How to delete graph 143
How to delete named print area 104
How to delete range 33
How to delete range name 34
How to delete rows 40
How to detach add-in 148
How to disable protection 45
How to display columns again 38
How to display embedded graph on full screen 144
How to display file list 39,124
How to display graph in color 144
How to display more rows 57
How to display named ranges 34
How to display page breaks 56
How to display WYSIWYG menu 147
How to draw a box 90
How to draw lines 89
How to edit formulas 32
How to edit graph 142
How to embed graph into the spreadsheet 141
How to enable the undo feature 50
How to enlarge cells 125% 58
How to enlarge cells 150% 58
How to enlarge cells a certain % 59

Table of Contents

How to enter absolute cell reference 48
How to enter numbers 31
How to enter the date 41
How to erase lines 90
How to erase range of cells 33
How to erase screen 25
How to erase worksheet 25
How to escape from menu 41
How to execute macros 165
How to extract unique entries only 161
How to find records in database 159
How to fix both titles 86
How to fix horizontal titles 86
How to fix vertical titles 85
How to format background color 88
How to format bold in WYSIWYG 87
How to format cell reference 68
How to format color for negative numbers 89
How to format commas 79
How to format currency 78
How to format date 42
How to format decimals 77
How to format dollar marks 78
How to format graph axes 133
How to format italics in WYSIWYG 87
How to format labels 62
How to format percentages 79
How to format range 77
How to format text color 88
How to format whole numbers 80
How to format worksheet 77
How to get command menu 21
How to get date 41

How to get help 27, 28
How to get maximum value 71
How to get menu 21
How to goto DOS 43
How to hide columns 38
How to hide zeros 86
How to import ASCII (text) 126
How to import WYSIWYG formats 149
How to insert columns 39
How to insert graphs into worksheet 141
How to insert rows 39
How to jump 44
How to jump to graph 142
How to jump to window 17
How to justify (wrap) cells 51
How to know the order of calculation 73
How to label column or row 61
How to label graph 145
How to left align cells 62
How to link spreadsheets 177
How to list files 26, 126
How to move around 18
How to move columns/rows 82
How to move range 37
How to move rows/cols 82
How to move to a window 17
How to move WYSIWYG formats 149
How to name a graph 134
How to name cell or range 33
How to name macro 163
How to name print settings 103
How to number pages 98
How to parse data 159

How to preview a spreadsheet before printing 114
How to print column borders on every page 101
How to print encoded file 107
How to print formulas 65
How to print frame 118
How to print graph 100, 137
How to print grid lines 118
How to print landscape 107
How to print more than one copy 117
How to print named range 98
How to print range 115
How to print row numbers on every page 102
How to print sample sheet of printer ability 105
How to print spreadsheet 26, 106
How to print to file 109
How to print using WYSIWYG 106
How to protect cells 44, 45
How to protect worksheet/cells 44, 45
How to put print job on hold 100
How to put the date in header 96
How to put the date and page # in header 97
How to query 154
How to quit Lotus 25
How to redisplay a column 38
How to release fixed titles 86
How to release synchronized scrolling 84
How to remove bold/italic 88
How to remove print job hold 100
How to remove shading 92
How to remove underlining 92
How to remove WYSIWYG formatting 91
How to replace words 26
How to replace words 52

How to replay macro 163
How to reset default layout 116
How to reset graph's settings 137
How to reset WYSIWYG to default print settings 118
How to retrieve a file 25, 121
How to right align words 62
How to save file 24, 121
How to save file under new name 123
How to save file with password 126
How to save graph 135
How to save new font set 64
How to save part of a spreadsheet 127
How to save to a floppy 123
How to save WYSIWYG formats 149
How to scroll both windows 84
How to scroll worksheet 41
How to search for data 159
How to select default printer 106
How to set advanced printer options 101
How to set black & white display 55
How to set cell size to normal 59
How to set color default 54
How to set colors 54
How to set graphics display 55
How to set line counter 99
How to set text attribute 65
How to shade areas in line graph 138
How to shade cells 91
How to solver circular reference errors 218
How to sort 43
How to sort rows 151
How to split column label into 2-3 lines 159
How to split the screen 83

Table of Contents

How to split titles 84
How to start a formula 67
How to start a new page 39,60
How to start Lotus 19
How to start printing from specific page 116
How to stop printing from a specific page 116
How to stop zeros from displaying 86
How to sum a column 70, 71
How to sum a row 71
How to suppress zeros 86
How to transfer data to another spreadsheet 125
How to transpose rows & columns 53
How to turn grid off on worksheet 56
How to turn grid on worksheet 55
How to turn recalculation back on 46
How to turn recalculation off 45
How to turn undo on or off 51
How to type aligned cell contents 19
How to type numbers 31
How to type words 26
How to underline 92
How to undo the last command 50
How to unhide column 38
How to unprotect worksheet/cells 45
How to unsplit windows 84
How to update data from another sheet 124
How to update default layout with custom 115
How to update default settings 58
How to update graphs 142
How to use #and# 74
How to use #or# 74
How to use @AVERAGE 71
How to use @COUNT 71

How to use @DATE 42
How to use @HLOOKUP 75
How to use @IF 72
How to use @NOW 41
How to use @SUM 69
How to use add-ins 213
How to use Auditor 217
How to use Backsolver 214
How to use function keys 19
How to use help 27, 28
How to use Icons 185, 219
How to use learn 164, 165
How to use macro library 215
How to use Macro Manager 215
How to use macro words 172
How to use macros 163
How to use math functions 69
How to use modes 20
How to use mouse 24, 28
How to use named graph 136
How to use operators 28
How to use parenthesis 73
How to use styles 93
How to use two key combination 27
How to use undo 50
How to use Viewer 216
How to use WYSIWYG 147
How to view graph 137
How to view saved graph 144
How to widen columns - all or several 59, 80
How to work with files 123
How to work with words 61
How to wrap words to several rows 51

Other Books Available or Coming Soon

<u>Available now</u> *
EASY INSTRUCTIONS FOR USING YOUR COMPUTER
$12.95   ISBN 1-880071-12-6

EASY INSTRUCTIONS FOR USING WORDPERFECT
$12.95   ISBN 1-880071-23-1

EASY INSTRUCTIONS FOR USING YOUR COMPUTER
(Spanish) $12.95   ISBN 1-880071-22-3

THE EASIEST BEGINNING COURSE ON HOW TO USE
YOUR COMPUTER $16.95   ISBN 1-880071-14-2

<u>Coming Soon</u> (1993)   Other handbooks $12.95 *

EASY INSTRUCTIONS ON HOW TO USE...
Windows . . . . ISBN 1-880071-09-6
Word . . . . ISBN 1-880071-10-X
Excel . . . . ISBN 1-880071-11-8

Contact your local dealer or bookstore. If they don't have them
ask them to get them.

* Prices subject to change.

Chapter 1 Getting Started

It is not my intention to cover absolutely every possible command option that Lotus has. There are too many for the average person. But this book covers the most common commands and then some. The average person that comes through my classes will never use all of the commands available. You do not need to know or use them all.

SOME BASICS

Help F1
Edit F2
Name cells F3
Absolute F4
Goto F5
Window F6
Query F7
Table F8
Calc F9
Graph F10
Compose characters Alt-F1
Run macro Alt-F3
Undo to last Ready mode Alt-F4
Learn range Alt-F5
Clear screen . . . . /WEY

Save   .... /FS
Retrieve file .... /FR
Print   .... /P
Copy cells .... /C

Correction keys

F2   - edits a cell
Backspace - moves one space to the left and deletes.
Delete   - deletes the character the cursor is on.
Insert   - toggles on Overtype mode so you can type and replace words.

Moving around

Jump:
to beginning of a spreadsheet . Home
to end of a spreadsheet ...... End-Home
end of row .... End-→
beginning of row .... End-←
next column .... →
top of range .... End-↑
bottom of range .... End-↓
column A .... End-←
last column .... End-→
up one screen .... PgUp
down one screen .... PgDn
right one screen .... tab
left one screen .... shift-tab
goto F5

To enter text (alpha) and cause alignment
1. press the character ' " or ^
2. type the text
3. Enter

'	apostrophe	left aligned text
"	quote	right aligned text
^	circumflex	centered
\	backslash	repeats character next typed
	across cell	

To get into Lotus - start it
1. be at the command line
2. type   C:
3. press Enter
4. type   CD \123R24 (or your own directory)
5. press Enter
6. type   123
7. press Enter

Function keys
F1	Help	will display help screen
F2	Edit	edits a cell contents
F3	Name	displays range of cells (in point mode)
F4	Absolute	changes relative cell ref to absolute
F5	Goto	jumps to whatever cell you type
F6	Window	jumps between two screen windows
F7	Query	repeats last data query
F8	Table	repeats last data table ??
F9	Recalc	recalculates all formulas

19

F10   Graph   displays currently defined graph

Used with Alt key (Hold Alt key and press function key):
F1   Compose   enters non-keyboard characters
F2   Step   runs macros stepping for finding errors
F3   Run   displays macros that can be run
F4   Undo   undoes changes since last Ready mode
F5   Learn   this turns on learn feature
F7   Program 1   runs optional add in program 1
F8   Program 2   runs optional add in program 2
F9   Program 3   runs optional add in program 3
F10   Prog menu   displays add in menu

Modes

A mode is the message on the upper right screen that tells you what state Lotus is in at the moment.

Edit   for editing a cell
Error   shows an error has happened. F1 gives help.
Files   list of files is showing
Find   means data query is being used to search
Frmt   you are editing a format line
Help   help screen is showing
Label   text is currently being entered
Menu   menu of commands is now showing
Names   range names, graph or add ins are on screen
Point   give a range
Ready   ready to enter data or label
Stat   a status screen is up

Value   entering value or formula

Wait   wait, Lotus is processing something (save, etc)

To see the commands menu

1. type the "/" (slash). It gives command menu at top screen.

2. move around menu by using arrows or type first letter of command name. Also, you can use downarrow to select option.

3. execute the menu option by hitting Enter.

WHAT IS A SPREADSHEET ?

Bookkeepers and accountants have used manual spreadsheets for years (actually centuries). Your checkbook is a good example.

On the left hand side of the paper, there is the date "column". Next is the check number and then the name of the person or company the check is made out to. All of these are in column format. Then there is the amount of the check. Finally you bring down the balance, this is also in a column.

A bookkeeper would then distribute the expenses into distribution columns. That just means they enter the amount a second time in another column depending on what kind of expense it was. If it was a check for office supplies, then the amount would be "posted" (written again) in the column designated as office supply expenses. This is so you can add up all the checks written and compare it to all the expenses broken down and distributed and they should match. It is also necessary for tax purposes to see what each check was written for. How much of what you spend went for rent, payroll, inventory, etc.

An accountant's bad dream is when the columns don't balance. You have to add them and re-add them checking each figure you posted to see where the mistake is. It could take a few minutes, hours, days, or even weeks to find the error(s).

BUDGET					
ITEM	CODE	SPENT	BUDGETED	DIFF	% OVER
Pens	101	58.95	75.00	16.05	21.4%
Pencils	102	142.33	125.00	−17.33	−13.9%
Paper	103	195.00	250.00	55.00	22.0%
Misc	104	280.00	300.00	20.00	6.7%
Salaries	105	5432.11	5000.00	−432.11	−8.6%
Rent	106	950.00	950.00		
Utilities	107	1456.23	1500.00	43.77	2.9%
Totals		$8,514.62	$8,200.00	($314.62)	−3.84%
Avg		1216.37	1171.43	−44.95	4.35%
Count		7			

Figure 1 A sample spreadsheet

A spreadsheet contains formulas in the places you want totals. Then you just plug in the amounts you spent and received and their disbursement code (what kind of expense they are) and they automatically post to the proper column and are added up correctly. No more hours or days searching for errors. Spreadsheets are great.

What you see on the screen is only a small part of the whole spreadsheet you are working with. You see through a window into part of it. You can move the view you see to anywhere in the spreadsheet you want. It's sort of like looking through binoculars.

23

You see 20 rows and 8 columns on the screen. Lotus is actually 8,192 rows by 256 columns wide. This is the equivalent of a sheet of paper 21 feet wide by 130 feet long.

To save a spreadsheet

Save your work every 10 minutes. It not only keeps you from losing your work but it is the best way to get yourself out of trouble. If you mess up your spreadsheet real bad, the easiest way out is to just erase the screen and retrieve the file the way it was saved 5 - 10 minutes ago. If you did not save recently, you could be facing a real mess and a lot of time to straighten it out.

Habits will either keep you out of trouble or get you in it!
1. press / F S
2. type the name of the spreadsheet
3. press Enter

If you already saved once
1. press / F S
2. press Enter
3. press R to overwrite the file

To use a Mouse with Lotus
1. install your mouse command software before entering Lotus.
2. use right mouse button to toggle between the two menus
3. click with left mouse button on any menu option as normal

Limits to filename

A Lotus file name can be up to 8 characters long. An example would be <u>Budget92</u> for a spreadsheet for 1992. Lotus will tag the file with a ".wk1" ending so I could tell all worksheet files from the rest.

To clear the screen
1. press /   for the menu up
2. press W   for Worksheet
3. press E   for Erase
4. press Y   for Yes I am sure

To retrieve a file
1. press /   for Menu
2. press F   for File
3. press R   for Retrieve
4. type the name of the file (or move to it)
5. press Enter

To quit Lotus
1. press /   for Menu
2. press Q   for Quit
3. press Y   for Yes

To print your spreadsheet
1. press /   for Menu
2. press P   for Print
3. press P   for Printer
4. press R   for Range (to tell it what part to print)
5. press .   and move to end of range
6. Enter
7. press G   for Go

To list files
1. press /   for Menu
2. press F   for Files
3. press L   for List
4. press W   for Worksheets (you can choose other kinds of files as well)

To type words
1. move to where you want to insert them
2. type them (they insert automatically)
3. Enter

To replace words
This keeps you from having to delete words first, then type new ones.

1. move to the words to replace
2. type new words (they replace old ones)
3. Enter

To get help
1. press F1
2. find the topic on the list that appears on the screen
3. scroll to it
4. Enter
 or
1. start the menu command you want help on
2. at the right option on the menu, press F1

It shows you help on that menu option.

To use a two key combination keystroke
1. hold down the first key, keep holding it
2. press the second key and release it quickly
3. then release the first key

Example: Alt-F3
You would hold down Alt, keep holding it, and then press
F3 quickly. Now let go of Alt.

To use a mouse

A mouse is a pointing device that you roll around on the desk and moves the pointer on the screen and click a button instead of pressing Enter.

• Install your mouse software before entering Lotus. Each mouse manufacturer could have different instructions for doing that. It could be as simple as typing Mouse. Some Pcs are set up to install the mouse command when you turn them on. Others, like mine, only install it when it is wanted.

1. press /   for Menu
2. point with the mouse
3. click left button

To get help with the mouse
1. click on the "?" on the right side of screen

Operators
+	addition
-	subtraction
/	division
*	multiplication
^	exponent
<	less than
>	greater than
<>	not equal to
=	equal to

#and# is the logical AND for two conditions used in IF's
#or# is the logical OR for either of two conditions

You can get help two ways in Lotus

1. press F1 anytime to get the Help Index of topics. You can then choose which topic to get help on.

2. get the menu of the subject you want help on, then press F1. It will give you specific help on that particular subject.

Chapter 2 The Worksheet

Entering numbers, text, & formulas
There are types of things you can enter into cells. These are numbers, text, and formulas.

To enter Numbers:
1. type the number
2. press an arrow key depending on where you're going

If you want to stay where you are after entering number, press Enter instead of the arrow.

To enter Text:
1. type text
2. press the arrow (or Enter).

No commands are necessary. If the text is wider than the cell, it spans to the next available cell to the right.

To enter formulas:
Method #1:
You can start your formula with any one of the following operators: + - ^ * / < >   But the + sign and the @ should be the most common ones you use.

1. type +
2. Use the Arrow key to move the cursor and highlight the first number to be used in the formula
3. type the operator between first number and second +/-
4. Use the Arrow key to move to second number
5. Repeat steps 2 & 3 until all numbers have been entered, hit Enter.

Method #2:
1. type +
2. type the cell address of first number (B3, etc).
3. type the operator between first number and second (+,-, *, / etc).
4. type second number (B4, etc).
5. Repeat step 3 & 4 until all numbers are entered.
6. press Enter

Don't forget F2 edits (if needed).

To attach an explanation to a number

You may want to make a notation to yourself about what this number does. If so, follow these steps.

1. type the number
2. type a semicolon (;) after the number
3. type the note
4. Enter

To name a range

A range is a group of cells (more than one). In many commands you are always telling Lotus which cells to do something to; that is, what is the range. It means from this cell to that cell.

1. press /   for Menu
2. press R   for Range
3. press N   for Name
4. press C   for Create
5. type name of range
6. Enter
7. type .
8. move to end of range
9. Enter

To erase a range (contents)

Erasing a cell deletes the contents of the cells. Those cell locations are still present on the worksheet. You cannot delete or erase the locations.

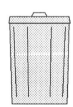

1. press /   for Menu
2. press R   for Range
3. press E   for Erase
4. move to beginning of range
5. type .
6. move to end of range
7. Enter

To erase one cell
1. press Delete key (in 2.3 or higher)
 or
1. press /   for Menu
2. press R   for Range
3. press E   for Erase
4. Enter twice

To display named ranges
You can assign a word name to a range (group of cells).
This means you can now refer to that word in commands
of all kinds instead of taking the time and effort to move
around all of the time from one cell location to another
telling Lotus the same location.

1. be doing any command where Lotus is in "point" mode
2. press F3   for List of names
3. move to range name wanted
4. Enter

To delete a range name
This would delete the name you assigned to a range and
not the contents of the cells.

1. press /   for Menu
2. press R   for Range
3. press N   for Name
4. press D   for Delete
5. scroll (move) to name to delete
6. Enter

To copy one cell to another cell

The copy command is one of the most common ones you will ever use. It is not hard but feels a little tricky at first. You should practice it a lot and get good at it.

1. move to cell you want to copy.
2. press /   for Menu
3. press C   for Copy
4. Enter
5. move to place to copy to
6. Enter

To copy one cell to other cells

A common example of this command is to add up (sum) one column and then copy this one cell formula to 6 other columns instead of remaking the same formula 6 more times.

1. move to cell you want to copy.
2. press /   for Menu
3. press C   for Copy
4. Enter
5. move to first cell to copy to.
6. type .
7. move to last cell to copy to
8. Enter

To copy a range

Copying a range is just like copying one cell except you highlight the group of cells to copy rather than it being just one. This command only copies the range to one other place, the next command copies to more than one place.

1. move to first cell in range to copy
2. press /   for Menu
3. press C   for Copy
4. move to end of range to copy
5. Enter
6. move to first cell in range to copy to
7. type .
8. move to end of range to copy to
9. Enter

To copy a range to more than one place

This command copies a group of cells (range) to more than one location (another range).

1. move to first cell in range to copy
2. press /   for Menu
3. press C   for Copy
4. move to end of range to copy
5. Enter
6. move to first cell in range to copy to.
7. type .
8. move to end of range to copy to.
9. Enter

Copying down

A very common and fast way to make formulas in a row is to make one, and copy it down to other rows.

1. press /   for Menu
2. press C   for Copy
3. Enter (if only copying one cell)
4. move to next row down.
5. type .
6. move to last row to copy to.
7. Enter

To move a range

This command will move a group of cells from one location to another.

1. move to first cell in range
2. press /   for Menu
3. press M   for Move
4. move to end of range
5. Enter
6. move to first cell in range to move to
7. Enter

How to hide columns

The purpose of hiding columns is usually to temporarily not show them so you can print certain columns that are not otherwise next to each other. Sometimes the reason is security. You may not want anyone else looking at your spreadsheet to see certain facts or figures.

1. press /   for Menu
2. press W   for Worksheet
3. press C   for Column, Enter
4. press H   for Hide, Enter
5. Enter   to ok current column

To redisplay column (unhide)

This command is to unhide columns you have used the Hide command on.

1. press /   for Menu
2. press W   for Worksheet
3. press C   for Column
4. press D   for Display
5. move to correct column and press
6. Enter

To display a full list of files
This command is different than /FR (File Retrieve). This command is for looking only. To retrieve or delete, use a different command under /F.

1. press   /   for Menu
2. press   F   for File
3. press   L   for List
4. to retrieve, move to file name
5. Enter

To start a new page (page break)
A page break tells the printer to start printing the next stuff on the next page.

1. move to row to start new page
2. press   /   for Menu
3. press   W   for Worksheet
4. press   P   for Page

Do not type anything else on this row.

To insert a blank row (or column)
You need the ability to move things around as we change our designs or outgrow our first design. Inserting rows for more transactions is one of the more common commands to do this.

1. press   /   for Menu
2. press   W   for Worksheet

3. press I   for Insert
4. press R   for Row
5. Enter

To insert several blank rows (or column)

1. press /   for Menu
2. press W   for Worksheet
3. press I   for Insert
4. press R   for Row
5. press .   for range
6. move to last row to show quantity to insert
7. Enter

To delete a row or column

This is the opposite of inserting one. The data on the row will be lost. The rows below it will move up to fill the void left. There will never be a gap between rows or columns.

1. move to row
2. press /   for Menu
3. press W   for Worksheet
4. press D   for Delete
5. press R   for Row
6. Enter

↑   represents the up arrow key
↓   represents the down arrow
→   represents the right arrow
←   represents the left arrow

To cancel a menu or command

Don't panic if you get in areas you don't mean to get in, or if you are just through with what you were doing and want to leave the menu. Press ESC in either of these situations.

press ESC

To scroll through a spreadsheet

Scrolling means to move using the arrows. You can scroll through a worksheet or a menu.

1. use PgDn or PgUp to move the view up or down
2. use tab or shift-tab to move right or left

To enter the date in a spreadsheet

This command will place the date in your spreadsheet. It is not just todays date but an ongoing command to bring the computer date into the sheet. Whenever you have the sheet on the screen in the future, that days date will appear, not the one from the day you did the command.

1. move cursor to place desired
2. type @Now or @today
3. Enter

You now have a serial date number needing formatting. A serial date is a sequential number that starts from January 1, 1990 with the number one. Every day since then adds one to this number. To make it change from a number in the tens of thousands to look like a real date, do the following command.

To enter any other date - @date
1. type @DATE(
2. type the year (2 digits, like: 93)
3. press comma (,)
4. type the month (2 digits, like: 07)
5. press comma (,)
6. type the day (2 digits, like: 11)
7. type)
8. Enter (a serial number is created)
9. then format it as below

Example: @DATE(93,01,12)
This would be January 12, 1993.

To format a date
4. press /   for Menu
5. press R   for Range
6. press F   for Format
7. press D   for Date
8. press 4   for Long International (or other)
9. Enter

To goto DOS

There may be many times you want to temporarily return to the DOS command line and do something without leaving Lotus. Your file stays open, your cursor stays where you left it and it is waiting for you to return. You might want to look for a file, format a floppy disk to put files on, or run a small program. Unless you are using Windows there won't be enough computer memory to run any large program without first completely leaving Lotus.

1. press /   for Menu
2. press S   for System
3. Do DOS commands
4. type Exit when done, Enter (returns you to Lotus)

To sort a list

Save your file first! Sorting a range of rows takes a lot of memory. I have heard a lot of wild stories from clients whose computers locked up or otherwise went nuts when they ran out of memory during a large sort. Also be sure to mark the entire row of data or Lotus will separate certain column entries from others. This is a Danger!! It can wreck your spreadsheet if separating them is not what you wanted.

1. move to first cell in area to sort
2. press /   for Menu
3. press D   for Data
4. press S   for Sort
5. press D   for Data-Range

6. press .   to start range
7. move to end of range (↓ and → to end of row)
8. Enter
9. press P   for Primary column
10. move to column to sort on
11. Enter
12. press A   for Ascending sort
13. Enter
14. press G   for GO

To jump to a certain cell area

Moving around with the arrow keys is fine for a small spreadsheet but if yours is getting large, moving becomes a pain in the neck. F5 can make that task easier. Just press F5 and tell it where you want to go and you fly there.

1. press F5
2. type the row and column to go to (like Z1000)
3. Enter

Protecting your formulas

Protecting cells from accidental erasure is a big concern to many people. Lotus allows you to have some cells protected and some not.

The procedure to accomplish this is twofold. First, you protect all the cells on the spreadsheet, and then unprotect the area you want able to be changed.

To protect the worksheet
1. press /   for Menu
2. press W   for Worksheet
3. press G   for Global
4. press P   for Protection
5. press E   for Enable

To unprotect individual cells
1. press /   for Menu
2. press R   for Range
3. press U   for Unprotect
4. move to first cell of range
5. press .
6. move to last cell of range
7. Enter
8. Repeat steps 4 - 7 for all ranges

To disable global protection
1. press /   for Menu
2. press W   for Worksheet
3. press G   for Global
4. press P   for Protection
5. press D   for Disable

To turn off recalculation
Sometimes as worksheets get larger they slow down. The type of computer and version of Lotus makes a difference. It slows down because Lotus recalculates all formulas that exist after you enter each new number or make each new formula. To turn off automatic recalculation and set it to

manual will speed up your data entry. That way you can key in data as fast as you can without any delay in getting your cursor back. If you want things to recalculate once in a while to see the results of you labor you can just press a key.

1. press /   for Menu
2. press W   for Worksheet
3. press G   for Global
4. press R   for Recalculation
5. press M   for Manual

To manually recalculate while recalc is off
Any time you want to see the results of your labor with updated formulas use this command.

1. press F9   for Recalc

To turn recalculation back on
To set it back to automatic.

1. press /   for Menu
2. press W   for Worksheet
3. press G   for Global
4. press R   for Recalculation
5. press A   for Automatic

Dangerous ways to make formulas

These are ways to get wrong numbers and not know it. If you make a formula and Lotus says ERR, that's good. It is letting you know you broke a serious rule. These 5 ways to danger are not breaking rules. Lotus would not have any way to know that you were not doing exactly what you intended to do. It will allow you to. You just won't get what you want.

1. Not using parentheses when needed. Parentheses are discussed soon in this book in the section on the Order of Calculation on page 73. You use them to group sets of numbers or cell locations and get them to execute first before the rest of the formula.

2. Not using absolute when needed. There are two ways to refer to a cells location. One is absolute and one is called relative. They are discussed on page 48.

3. Moving columns or rows. When you move rows and columns around, sometimes it could mess up your formulas. Lotus is pretty good at rewriting your formulas automatically when you make changes like inserting rows or columns. But sometimes, under certain conditions, with certain formulas, they could be wrong. This is a warning that it is possible for this to happen and to recheck your formulas for accuracy after moving, deleting or inserting rows or columns.

4. Deleting columns or rows. This goes along with danger number three.

5. Not including the entire column range in a column total is a big danger. This is very real even though some of my students have already gotten rigid in their habits before coming to our classes. When you make a formula that sums a column, make the range go all the way to the line you drew right before the total formulas for the columns. This way when you fill in new row entries, they will increase the total of the column. If you don't do this and others fill in the spreadsheet data, they won't know you didn't include those new rows they are entering data on and the column total would not be right. It could be off a few dollars, hundreds, thousands, or even millions depending on what you do.

Absolute cell references vs relative

There are two ways to make formulas, Absolute or Relative. The first way, Absolute, refers to a value that is constant. Relative formulas are variable.

Example:
To calculate how much printing was of our total expenses for the month, we divide the amount spent on printing by the total expenses on everything. To find out what percent postage was, we do the same thing. Printing and postage are variables, and would be expressed in relative terms in a formula. The total amount spent would be the same for each formula so it needs to be expressed as an absolute.

Since pointing with the arrows is the easiest way to make formulas no matter which kind you need, Lotus has an easy way to convert relative expressions to absolute so we can use the arrows 100% of the time.

To convert a relative cell reference to absolute
Most of the time in making a formula the cell references you make are relative. Once in a while you need one to be absolute. Formulas can contain both relative and absolute cell references.

1. move to highlight the cell to be in the formula
2. press F4 function key

A formula of +B11-C12 in which the C12 needed to be Absolute would now look like this after conversion: +B11-C12. The dollar signs indicate an absolute reference.

Absolute cell reference Example:
To make a formula in a row that would figure the percent of total payroll for each employee would have one relative cell reference in it and one absolute.

1. press +   to start the formula
2. move left to the cell with the employees gross amount
3. press /   for divide by
4. move to the cell that is the total for the gross column
5. press F4   for Absolute

6. Enter
7. now copy it down to the other rows in that column

How to place sequence numbers

A Data Fill is another name for sequence numbers. These numbers start with a certain number and increment by some quantity you tell it. You could start a monthly listing of invoice numbers by doing this command. You would answer the questions which number to start with, how many to add to it to get the next number, and what number to stop with. You can even increment dates this way. Type in the first date, which gives a large serial number. Then do a Fill command. Then format the whole range for dates.

1. press /   for Menu
2. press D   for Data
3. press F   for Fill
4. move to beginning of range
5. type   .
6. move to end of range, Enter
7. type the # to start, Enter
8. type the # to increase each number by
9. type sequence number to stop with
10. Enter

To Undo the last command

Undo is a great feature that lets us change our minds about the last command we did or correct our mistakes if we realize we should not have done what we just did.

1. look to be sure "Undo" is at the bottom of the screen
2. press Alt-F4

To set up the ability to use Undo

This command is usually done once. It enables the use of Undo which will reverse the action of the last command, even if it was erasing the worksheet without saving. If Undo is not showing at the bottom of the screen, you cannot execute it. Lotus comes with this feature as an option, not set to use.

1. press /   for Menu
2. press W   for Worksheet
3. press G   for Global
4. press D   for Default
5. press O   for Other
6. press U   for Undo
7. press E   for Enable
   THEN
8. press /   for Menu
9. press W   for Worksheet
10. press G   for Global
11. press D   for Default
12. press U   for Update

To word wrap column headings (any text)

Sometimes column headings are long and should be placed in several cells above each other rather than widen a column that does not need to be widened just for small numbers.

1. press /   for Menu
2. press R   for Range
3. press J   for Justify
4. Enter

• You can do a range rather than the cell where you are.

Example:

"This is a test column heading" would look like this after wrapping it:

This is a
test column
heading

To search & replace in a range

This command is similar to a word processing feature. It lets you search a range of cells looking for a word, phrase or number. When it is found be automatically replaced by a different word, phrase or number. You tell it which cells to look in as well as what to search for and replace with.

1. press /   for Menu
2. press R   for Range
3. press S   for Search
4. move to the first cell of range
5. press .
6. move to last cell of range
7. type the words to search for

8. press L   for Labels (or Formulas or Both)
9. press R   for Replace (or F for only Find)
10. type the words to replace with
11. Enter
12. press A   for All (or Replace this one, or Next)

To switch (transpose) rows & columns

We don't always design our spreadsheets the best way the first time. So later we may wish a column we made was actually a row or the other way around. No problem, we can switch it. This is called Transpose.

1. press /   for Menu
2. press R   for Range
3. press T   for Transpose
4. move to first cell of range
5. press .
6. move to last cell of range
7. Enter
8. move to first cell of where to put it
9. Enter

WYSIWYG Menu options

To set colors

Setting colors and other such commands are not available on the normal Lotus menu. You must install the WYSIWYG add-in discussed later and use that command menu. This is an extra power feature of Lotus that is very good. Use it. It is only available with 2.3 version of Lotus or higher.

1. press :   for Menu
2. press D   for Display
3. press C   for Colors
4. press B   for Background
5. choose a color
6. press T   for Text
7. choose a color
8. press the first letter of any other option
9. choose it's color
10. press Q   for Quit when done
11. press Q   for Quit again

To make the new colors default (automatic)

The default is the way you want Lotus to be all the time.

1. press :   for Menu
2. press D   for Display
3. press D   for Default
4. press U   for Update

To change between graphics and text display
Usually the reason to change this is because of the type of monitor you have.

1. press :   for Menu
2. press D   for Display
3. press M   for Mode
4. press G   for Graphic (T for text)
5. press Q   for Quit

To change to Black & White/Color display
Black & white may be easier for some people with trouble seeing certain colors. It might be better because you have a monochrome monitor.

1. press :   for Menu
2. press D   for Display
3. press M   for Mode
4. press B   for Black & White (C for color)

To turn the Grid on
A Grid is a background set of lines that run between each column and each row. It makes it easier for some people to see what numbers fall in which rows. This idea is like the bookkeeping ledger paper that so many people have used for years. You can then choose to print with the grids or without. You can use them on the screen and not have to print them out or the other way around.

1. press :   for Menu

2. press D   for Display
3. press O   for Options
4. press G   for Grid
5. press Y   for Yes

To turn the Grid off
1. press :   for Menu
2. press D   for Display
3. press O   for Options
4. press G   for Grid
5. press N   for No

To display Page-Breaks
1. press :   for Menu
2. press D   for Display
3. press O   for Options
4. press P   for Page-breaks
5. press Y   for Yes

To change the appearance of the Frame
The Frame is the area around the top and left of the screen that shows the column letters and row numbers.

1. press :   for Menu
2. press D   for Display
3. press O   for Options
4. press F   for Frame
5. choose what to change

To change the Cell-Pointer to a hollow outline
This is another option that some people may prefer. Many of the commands under WYSIWYG are options.

1. press :   for Menu
2. press D   for Display
3. press O   for Options
4. press C   for Cell-pointer
5. press O   for Outline

To change the display to bright
There are two intensities on a screen. One is normal, the other is bright. Bright appears to be about twice as bright as normal.

1. press :   for Menu
2. press D   for Display
3. press O   for Options
4. press I   for Intensity
5. press H   for High

To display more rows at one time
The normal screen is 80 characters (character columns) wide by 25 rows high. Lotus lets you change the row display to fit more rows on the screen viewing area. Or less rows to make the type bier.

1. press :   for Menu
2. press D   for Display
3. press R   for Rows

57

4. type a number from 16 to 60
5. Enter

To update the Default settings

The default is the way you want Lotus to be set when you start a new sheet. You don't want to have to make your favorite changes each time you start a new sheet. This command lets you save those changes.

1. press :   for Menu
2. press D   for Display
3. press D   for Default
4. press U   for Update

To enlarge worksheet cells 125%

This is another command that lets you change the size of the cells - enlarge cells - and writing on the screen. People with less than normal vision will appreciate this.

1. press :   for Menu
2. press D   for Display
3. press Z   for Zoom
4. press L   for Large

To enlarge worksheet cells 150%

1. press :   for Menu
2. press D   for Display
3. press Z   for Zoom
4. press H   for Huge

To enlarge worksheet cells a certain %
This sets a certain % up or down for cell size.
1. press :   for Menu
2. press D   for Display
3. press Z   for Zoom
4. press M   for Manual
5. type a number from 25 to 400
6. Enter

To set cell size to normal
If you ever want to set the size of cells back to normal size, this command does it.

1. press :   for Menu
2. press D   for Display
3. press Z   for Zoom
4. press N   for Normal

To set the width of columns
Columns by default of Lotus are 9 characters wide. There are many times this is not adequate for certain columns. Usually column A is a description column of some kind and needs more than 9 characters. One of my most common settings is 25 characters for this first column. The standard Lotus menu also has a command that will do this, you don't need WYSIWYG.

1. press :   for Menu
2. press W   for Worksheet
3. press C   for Column

4. press S   for Set width
5. move to the first column to widen
6. press .
7. move to last column to widen
8. Enter
9. type a quantity from 1 to 240
10. Enter

To set a page break
You can do this in the normal Lotus menu as well.

1. press :   for Menu
2. press W   for Worksheet
3. press P   for Page
4. press R   for Row (or C for vertical)
5. press Q   for Quit

To clear a page break
This is another command available in the normal menu. If you want to erase a page break, do this.

1. press :   for Menu
2. press W   for Worksheet
3. press P   for Page
4. press D   for Delete
5. press Q   for Quit

Chapter 3 Words

When you type words, they are entered into the cell where you are located. If you type more than can fit into one cell, the words flow over into the next cells to the right if they are empty. If they are not empty, the words are still held behind the scenes but do not display.

If you ever delete what is in the cell next to you or widen the column the words are in, they will now show.

To label columns or rows

You will need to title the tops of your columns and insert descriptions in row 1 (or whichever), telling you and anyone else who sees your spreadsheet what each column is and what each entry represents.

To align your label, precede it with one of the following:

1. an apostrophe: '   for left-aligned label
2. a quotation mark   "   for right-aligned label
3. a caret symbol   ^   for centered label
4. a backslash   \   for repeating label

If you don't choose one, the default is left aligned text, and right aligned numbers.

Left aligned	Right aligned	Centered

A repeated label will be the same character put across the cell, like:

```
--------------------
```

Example 1:
To place the label at the top of a column and center it:
1. move to the correct cell.
2. type ^Amt Enter
3. Step 2 places the word "Amt" in the cell and centers it.

You could also have type several column headings and then do a Range Format command on all of them at the same time.

Example 2:
To place -'s across the whole cell:
1. move to cell.
2. type \- Enter

Step 2 places "-"'s across the whole cell.

WYSIWYG Menu commands

To change Font (shape & size)
A font is a typestyle of a certain size. The size (height) of a font is expressed in points. A point is 1/72 of an inch. 10 point type is equal to Elite type. 12 point type is the same size as Pica. 36 points would be half an inch.

1. press :   for Menu
2. press F   for Format
3. press F   for Font
4. type a number from 1 to 8
5. Enter
6. press .   for the range
7. move to end of range
8. Enter

To change Font selections in the set of 8
Lotus gives you a set of 8 fonts to be a standard to choose from. If you want to change one or more of the 8 in the set to something else, use this command.

1. press :   for Menu
2. press F   for Format
3. press F   for Font
4. press R   for Replace
5. type a number from 1 to 8
6. press O   for Other
7. scroll the list of fonts

8. Enter to choose one
9. type a number up to 72 for point size
10. Enter
11. press Q   for Quit

To save the new Font selections in the set

If you want a permanent change in the choice of the 8 fonts in your set, use this command. If you want it for this spreadsheet only, don't use this command.

1. press :   for Menu
2. press F   for Format
3. press F   for Font
4. press D   for Default
5. press U   for Update

WYSIWYG Menu commands

To align text across cells

You would use this command to center a title across the top of your screen. You could also use it to center (right or left align also) any words across any group of cells.

1. press :   for Menu
2. press T   for Text
3. press A   for Align
4. press C   for Center (or Left, Right, Even)

5. move to first cell of range
6. press .
7. move to last cell of range
8. Enter

To set text attribute for cells

This will format the cells to show formulas or other data as alpha text rather than the result of formulas. This is used sometimes in database query so when you print the output of the query it also shows what search formula was used to get it.

1. press   :   for Menu
2. press   T   for Text
3. press   S   for Set
4. move to first cell of range
5. press .
6. move to last cell of range
7. Enter

To clear the text attribute from cells

If you no longer want the cells formatted like the command above, use this command to reset them.

1. press   :   for Menu
2. press   T   for Text
3. press   C   for Clear
4. move to first cell of range
5. press .

6. move to last cell of range
7. Enter

Chapter 4   Formulas

Start a formula with

The most common two ways to start a formula is with the + or the @. Use the + when there will not be any special Function words used (like Sum). Use the @ before each Function word that begins a formula.

+
@
-
.
(
$

Arithmetic functions

These signs can be used in a formula just like on a calculator. Never put any spaces in a formula.

+   add
-      subtract
*   multiply
/   divide
^   exponent

Logical functions

These symbols can also be used in a formula to compare two cells and tell Lotus what to do if a certain condition is met.

=	equals
<	less than
>	grcatcr than
<=	less than or equal to
>=	greater than or equal to
<>	not equal to
#and#	used in formula to make two conditions true
#or#	used in formula to make either condition true
#not#	not true test

Cell reference formats

A cell reference is a way to refer to a cell. You can either tell Lotus to go one cell to the left (for example) and one cell up to get a number. You could copy this any where else on the sheet and it would do the same command but from its new location. The other way is to tell it exactly where a cell is you want to do something with, like C3 and nowhere else.

A1	absolute column and absolute row
A$1	relative column and absolute row
$A1	absolute column and relative row
A1	relative column and relative row

Math functions

Function	Format
@IF	
states a condition.	@IF(test,do,else)
@SUM	
adds column or row.	@SUM(uparrow.downarrow)
@AVG	
avgs a range.	@AVG(uparrow .
downarrow)	
@COUNT	
counts transactions.	@COUNT(uparrow .
downarrow)	
@TODAY	
puts todays date.	@TODAY
@CHAR	
types ASCII character	@CHAR(171) for example
@DATE	
places any date	@DATE(yr,mo,day)

* There are many others not covered here.

To add two cells together

This is an example of a "simple formula". No special Function words are used and the cells referred to could be 10 or more instead of just 2.

1. move to where you want the answer to show
2. type + to start formula
3. move to the first cell to add
4. type + to put it's location in formula
5. move to the next cell to add
6. Enter

• Either start your formula with a "+"

To sum a column

Adding a column or row is the most common formula most spreadsheet users make. You add one, then copy it to the other rows or columns nearby.

1. move cursor to where you want the total to show.
2. type @SUM(
3. Use uparrow to move to first cell in range to add.
4. press the period.
5. Use downarrow to move to last cell in range to add.
6. press)
7. Enter

To sum a row
1. move cursor to where you want the total to show
2. type @SUM(
3. Use arrow to move to first cell in range to add
4. press .
5. Use arrow to move to last cell in range to add
6. press)
7. Enter

To average a column
You get the average of a range, the count, maximum value, and minimum value the same way you sum it.

1. move cursor to where you want the total to show.
2. type @AVG(
3. Use uparrow to move to first cell in range.
4. press the period.
5. Use downarrow to move to last cell in range.
6. press)
7. Enter

To count how many entries in a column
This command would count the number of entries it took to get a certain total. Sometimes depending on what you are counting, you are best to count on a column that has keyed in numbers rather than computed in case some computed cells are empty, thus throwing off the answer.

1. move cursor to where you want the total to show.
2. type @COUNT(

3. Use uparrow to move to first cell in range
4. press the period.
5. Use downarrow to move to last cell in range
6. press)
7. Enter

To create an If condition

An if condition is one of the most powerful ways to make a formula. To get good at a spreadsheet, get good at making if conditions. You basically tell Lotus to look at something and compare it to something else. Based on the answer to the comparison, you either do the first instruction I'm going to tell you or the second.

1. type @IF(
2. type or move to create condition (like A2<1000)
3. type a comma
4. type or move to create Do expression
5. type a comma
6. type or move to create Else expression
7. press)
8. Enter

Correcting mistakes

To edit your mistakes:

1. move cursor to cell you want to correct.
2. Hit the F2 function key.
3. Use left and right arrows to move within the contents of the cell that are displayed in the upper left part of your screen.

4. Use Backspace, Delete, and type what you DO want to make the corrections.

5. When finished editing, press Downarrow or Enter to place

Note: The HOME-→and END-← keys do jump you to the beginning or end of the line you're editing.

Order of calculation (precedence)

( )   1st
^   2nd
* /   3rd
+ -   4th

ORDER OF CALCULATION

Lotus calculates numbers in a certain order. It doesn't vary from this order. This is a possible danger zone for you. You must make your formulas according to how it is going to calculate. It works from column one row one down the column. Then it goes to the next column. You can change this order if you are advanced and want certain types of spreadsheets, but most people do not.

The order of calculation is:

( )   first
* /   second
+ -   third

Example 1:

5 + 3 * 2 = 16   calculated by hand.

5 + 3 * 2 = 11   calculated by Lotus.

When you calculate the formula in Example 1 by hand, you know to add the first two numbers before multiplying the third. Lotus doesn't know to do that. It's order of execution is to multiply and divide before it adds and subtracts. With that in mind, it first multiplied the 3 x 2 and got 6. Then it added the 5 to the 6 and got 11, which is not right, if you wanted it to calculate from left to right which most people do under most conditions. See how it makes a big difference.

How do we tell Lotus to add first? We use parentheses. Lotus does anything in parentheses before it even multiplies or divides. So, doing this our new way to write the formula so Lotus knows what we want is:

(5 + 3) * 2 = 16

Now Lotus will add what's in parentheses first and get 8. Then it will multiply the 8 x 2 and get 16. That is the correct answer.

And/Or formulas
You can use #and# and #or# in a formula to put two conditions in an if statement.

Example: If(B2>30#and#B2<60,B2,0)

This would look at the age of an invoice (for instance) and see if it was greater than 30 days <u>and</u> less than 60 days.

<u>#AND#</u> would need both conditions met to be true, <u>#OR#</u> would only need either condition met to be true.

To make a lookup table

A lookup table is just what it says. It is a series of rows and columns that have incremental numbers (usually). You can use it to look up a value and when that value is found, go to another column and pull a value from that column and do something with it. A UPS chart of shipping charges would be a good example.

@Vlookup   used for vertical tables
@Hlookup   used for horizontal tables

1. move to an unused area of the worksheet off to the right of you work area
2. type the columns and rows of data that make the table
3. move to the spot to make the lookup formula (it will not be in the table itself but somewhere else that you want to put the answer to the lookup).

 Now you are ready to make the formula:
4. type @Vlookup(
5. type the number or cell location to look up in the table
6. type a comma
7. type the range that makes up the table to search
8. type a comma

9. type the number of columns from the first that the
column with the answer is found
10. type)
11. Enter

Example of table:

Sales	Discount
100	.02
200	.03
300	.04
400	.05
500	.06

Example of lookup formula:
@Vlookup(G6,R4..S8,1)

This example looks up the value in G6 in the table located
in the area R4..S8. Then it looks one column to the right
and pulls that value on the same row as the match that
was found.

Chapter 5 Formatting

Formatting is one of the main command areas you will do a lot. It is how you get dollar marks, commas, percent signs, dates, and more. The default settings for Lotus are called General. It means words are left aligned in the cell, numbers are right aligned. It also means that numbers will display the format of whatever the number actually is. That means a whole number, like 25, will display just 25. The number 3.21 will display 3.21. If it was 45.2 then 45.2 will display. The number 4.32145 will display just like that. To get these numbers to look any other way, you must format them.

The use of formatting never affects the accuracy of the number.

To format 2 decimals for a range
This command will make all numbers in the range look like 41.23. Two decimal places past the period will show. The number 32.123 will display 32.12. The number 25 will display 25.00.

1. press /   for Menu
2. press R   for Range
3. press F   for Format
4. press F   for Fixed
5. press 2   for 2 decimals

6. Enter
7. move to 1st cell to format
8. press .
9. move to last cell to format
10. Enter

To format 2 decimals for whole spreadsheet
1. press /   for Menu
2. press W   for Worksheet
3. press G   for Global
4. press F   for Format
5. press F   for Fixed
6. press 2   for 2 decimals
7. Enter
8. move to 1st cell to format
9. press .
10. move to last cell to format
11. Enter

To format dollar marks
This will set both dollar marks and the decimals you want at the same time. The number 3.2 becomes $3.20.

1. move to beginning of range to have $
2. press /   for Menu
3. press R   for Range
4. press F   for Format
5. press C   for Currency
6. press 2   for 2 decimals
7. Enter

8. move to the end of range to have $
9. Enter

To format percent signs (%)

In using percentages, in most cases people like to set either no decimals or one. You can set whatever you or your boss want. The number .1678 formatted for one decimal becomes 16.8%. The number .03222 becomes 3.2%. And finally 1.234 becomes 102.3%. The number one (1) becomes 100%. The accuracy of the number is not affected by formatting.

1. move to beginning of range to have %
2. press /   for Menu
3. press R   for Range
4. press F   for Format
5. press P   for Percent
6. press 2   for 2 decimals
7. Enter
8. move to the end of range to have %
9. Enter

To format commas

Using this format will cause commas to be displayed as well as set the number of decimals you want. The number 2345.1 becomes 2,245.10 if set for two decimals.

1. move to beginning of range to have commas
2. press /   for Menu
3. press R   for Range

4. press F   for Format
5. press ,   for Commas
6. press 2   for 2 decimals
7. Enter
8. move to the end of range to have commas
9. Enter

To format whole numbers
This command will drop any decimals and display only whole integer numbers.

1. move to beginning of range
2. press /   for Menu
3. press R   for Range
4. press F   for Format
5. press ,   for Commas
6. press 0   for 0 decimals
7. Enter
8. move to the end of range
9. Enter

To change column width
You can set this command here of in WYSIWYG.

1. press /   for Menu'
2. press W   for Worksheet
3. press C   for Column
4. press S   for Set-Width

5. press → until the column is wide enough
   (or key in quantity)
6. Enter

To change all columns width

If you have a project that requires most numbers to be large, and together with the room allowed for formatting will be more than 9 characters, you can change the whole spreadsheet in one command.

1. press /   for Menu
2. press W   for Worksheet
3. press G   for Global
4. press C   for Column width
5. key in the width you want
6. Enter

To change several columns width

This command changes more than one column at the same time but not the entire spreadsheet.

1. press /   for Menu
2. press W   for Worksheet
3. press C twice   for Column-range
4. press S   for Set-width
5. press .
6. move to the last column to widen
7. Enter
8. key in quantity, then Enter

How to move rows & columns

When you move columns and rows, be sure and recheck your formulas to be sure they are still accurate. Under most conditions they will be. Sometimes they might not be depending on what you are doing and how you made your formulas.

1. move to row or column to move.
2. press /   for Menu
3. press M   for Move

If only moving one:
4. Enter
5. move to where you want it.
6. Enter   (the column or row moves)

If moving more than one:
4. type .
5. move to end of range.
6. Enter
7. move to where you want it.
8. Enter (the column/row range moves)

Deleting rows & columns

Recheck your formulas for accuracy after doing this command.

1. move to column or row to delete.
2. press /   for Menu
3. press W   for Worksheet

4. press D   for Delete
5. press R or C for Row or Column
6. Enter (be sure you have moved to the one to delete)

How to split the screen
You may need to view two areas of the worksheet at the same time. There could be the need to look at the totals on rows 100-105 to see how they change when you enter transactions on rows 35-50. Especially with a model worksheet, like a budget, you might find this useful to do some what if. You can make some changes to the data and see how it affects the totals.

1. press HOME to view beginning area
2. move to where you want to split
3. press /   for Menu
4. press W   for Worksheet
5. press W   for Window
6. press H   for Horizontal
7. press F6   function key to change windows.

To close window
When you are done with the split screen this is how to get back to one whole screen.

1. press /   for Menu
2. press W   for Worksheet
3. press W   for Window
4. press C   for Clear

To scroll both windows together
When split Horizontally, windows scroll left and right together. When Vertical, windows scroll up and down together.

1. press /   for Menu
2. press W   for Worksheet
3. press W   for Window
4. press S   for Sync

To release synchronized scrolling
When you no longer want split screens to be synchronized but to scroll independently do this command.

1. press /   for Menu
2. press W   for Worksheet
3. press W   for Window
4. press U   for Unsync

To fix titles that can always be seen
This command will lock the row headings and a few other rows if wanted so that no matter how far down the spreadsheet you go you can still see the column headings. If you don't do this, then when you go down past row 30 or so you will not be able to see the column headings anymore. They will scroll off the top of the screen. You may have trouble now telling which column is which unless your data is either small or very obvious.

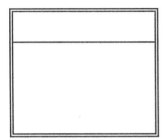

1. move to the row where you want to split the screen
2. press /   for Menu
3. press W   for Worksheet
4. press T   for Titles
5. press H   for Horizontal

To fix vertical titles

This command is usually done to lock the columns of description from scrolling off the screen to the left when you move to the right to more columns. With vertical titles split you can go to column 100 and still see the description for the rows in the first column or two. Without this command, you may not be able to tell what row is for what.

1. move to the column where you want to split
2. press /   for Menu
3. press W   for Worksheet
4. press T   for Titles
5. press V   for Vertical

To fix both horizontal & vertical titles

This command splits both vertical and horizontal titles at one time with just one command. Be sure and move to the spot for splitting both rows and columns.

1. press /   for Menu
2. press W   for Worksheet
3. press T   for Titles
4. press B   for Both

To release titles

To clear titles when you do not need them split anymore use this command. If you have strange printing problems you might try removing this command and then printing. It has been known to interfere depending on which version of Lotus you have and which printer.

1. press /   for Menu
2. press W   for Worksheet
3. press T   for Titles
4. press C   for Clear

To not display zero values

Sometimes when you copy formulas to other cells they will produce a zero value. If you do not want these zeros to show or print, then use this command.

1. press /   for Menu
2. press W   for Worksheet
3. press G   for Global

4. press Z   for Zero
5. press Y   for Yes (N on some wrong versions)

WYSIWYG Menu options

Using WYSIWYG you can make words or numbers
format just like in a word processor. Bold, underline,
italics, font size, and more are all possible.

To make cell contents Bold (or other)
1. press :   for Menu
2. press F   for Format
3. press B   for Bold
4. press S   for Set
5. press .   for the range
6. move to end of range to bold
7. Enter

To make cell contents Italic
1. press :   for Menu
2. press F   for Format
3. press I   for Italic
4. press S   for Set
5. press .   for the range
6. move to end of range to bold
7. Enter

To remove Bold from cells
1. press :   for Menu
2. press F   for Format
3. press B   for Bold
4. press C   for Clear
5. press .   for the range
6. move to end of range
7. Enter

To format text color to see and print
This command changes the color of just the writing on the screen.

1. press :   for Menu
2. press F   for Format
3. press C   . for Color
4. press T   for Text
5. choose a color
6. press .   for the range
7. move to end of range
8. Enter

To format background color to see and print
This command changes the background color of the screen but not the writing.

1. press :   for Menu
2. press F   for Format
3. press C   for Color
4. press B   for Background

5. choose a color
6. press   .   for the range
7. move to end of range
8. Enter

To color for negative numbers to see and print

You can make negative numbers show in a different color just like on a calculator or adding machine. This is for easier identification.

1. press   :   for Menu
2. press   F   for Format
3. press   C   for Color
4. press   N   for Negative
5. choose a color
6. press   .   for the range
7. move to end of range
8. Enter

To draw lines

The draw lines command has many options. You can draw single lines, double or thick. You can put them under a cell(s) over around or whatever.

1. press   :   for Menu
2. press   F   for Format
3. press   L   for Lines
4. press   a letter for (Right, Top, Bottom, etc)
5. press   .   for the range

6. move to end of range
7. Enter

To draw a box around cells
1. press :   for Menu
2. press F   for Format
3. press L   for Lines
4. press O   for Outline
5. press .   for the range
6. move to end of range
7. Enter

To erase lines around cells
1. press :   for Menu
2. press F   for Format
3. press L   for Lines
4. press C   for Clear
5. press a letter for (Outline, left, ...)

To make a shadow box around cells
A shadow box is also called a drop shadow. It looks like a white box with writing in it and to two sides is a black, thick line a little shorter than the box. It gives the appearance of a shadow to one side of the box. This command is used a lot in advertising and desktop publishing.

1. press :   for Menu
2. press F   for Format
3. press L   for Lines

4. press S   for Shadow
5. press S   for Set
6. press .   for the range
7. move to end of range
8. Enter

To remove WYSIWYG formatting

This does not remove any other formatting from the Range
menu or Worksheet.

1. press :   for Menu
2. press F   for Format
3. press R   for Reset

To shade cells

Shading means to put a background gray behind cells. You
can set the percentage of shade to have. Set it light or your
text may be hard to read when printed.

1. press :   for Menu
2. press F   for Format
3. press S   for Shading
4. press L   for Light
5. press .   for the range
6. move to end of range
7. Enter

To remove shading
1. press :   for Menu
2. press F   for Format
3. press S   for Shading
4. press C   for Clear
5. press .   for the range
6. move to end of range
7. Entcr

To underline cells
This command is different than drawing lines. It is true underlining like a word processor.

1. press :   for Menu
2. press F   for Format
3. press U   for Underline
4. press S   for Single (D for Double...)
5. press .   for the range
6. move to end of range
7. Enter

To remove underlining in cells
1. press :   for Menu
2. press F   for Format
3. press U   for Underline
4. press C   for Clear
5. press .   for the range
6. move to end of range
7. Enter

This won't work on empty cells. Use the (:FL) Format Lines command to underline empty cells.

To create a Named-Style (Define style)

A style is a collection of format settings that has been assigned a name. You can then highlight cells and choose a style to apply to them and save many commands and aggravation in repeating steps.

1. press :   for Menu
2. press N   for Named-Style
3. press D   for Define
4. press a number from 1 to 8 to assign style
5. move to cell with formatting set
6. Enter
7. backspace out the name "normal"
8. type new name for this style
9. Enter
10. type style description (optional)
11. Enter

To use Styles

Once a style is created like above, this command is how you apply them to highlighted cells.

1. press :   for Menu
2. press N   for Named-Style
3. press a number from 1 to 8 for style wanted
4. move to first cell in range to apply style to
5. press .

6. move to last cell in range
7. Enter

Chapter 6 Printing

To print your spreadsheet

1. press /   for Menu
2. press P   for Print
3. press P   for Printer
4. press R   for Range (to tell it what part to print)
5. press .   and move to end of range
6. Enter
7. press G   for Go

To change margins

Margins are the non-printed border areas around the sheet of paper. The default is 1 inch.

1. press /   for Menu
2. press P   for Print
3. press P   for Printer
4. press O   for Options
5. press M   for Margins
6. press L   for Left (or R,T, or B)
7. type   # of characters, Enter
8. press Q   for Quit
9. press Q   for Quit

To create a header
A header is a line or two of text that will print at the top of each page. The name of a report and the date would be good to put in a header.

1. press /   for Menu
2. press P   for Print
3. press P   for Printer
4. press O   for Options
5. press H   for Header
6. type the line for header, Enter
7. press Q   for Quit
8. press Q   for Quit

In placing header, use one vertical bar (Shift-\) to center the header. Two would divide the header into thirds.

To put the date automatically in header
This command will bring up the date differently depending on the day you retrieve the worksheet and print it. It does not just hold the date of the day you create it.

1. create header as above
2. type the @ where you want it to appear

To put page numbering in header
1. create header as above
2. type the # where you want it to appear

To put the date and page number in a header
1. create header as above
2. type @
3. type the vertical bar (|)
4. type #

It looks like this: @|Page #

Results look like this: January 1, 1993   Page 1

To create a footer
A footer is a line or two of text that appears at the bottom of each page.

1. press /   for Menu
2. press P   for Print
3. press P   for Printer
4. press O   for Options
5. press F   for Footer
6. type the line for footer, Enter
7. press Q   for Quit
8. press Q   for Quit

In placing footer, use one vertical line (|) to center the footer. Use Shift-\ to get this symbol. Two would divide the footer into thirds. The @ places today's date.

To number pages in footer
1. press / for Menu
2. press P for Print
3. press P for Printer
4. press O for Options
5. press F for Footer
6. type |# for number, Enter
7. press Q for Quit
8. press Q for Quit

To change the size of print
It depends on your Lotus version and printer as to whether you will ever use this command. With new printers on the market with increased ability and WYSIWYG you may never use it.

1. press / for Menu
2. press P for Print
3. press P for Printer
4. press O for Options
5. press S for Setup
6. type the setup string   (like \015 for IBM or Epson for compressed print - see your   own printer manual)
7. press Q for Quit
8. press Q for Quit (G for Go)

To print named range
If you print an area of your spreadsheet often, it would save time and effort if you named that area. Then at time of printing just refer to the name and that area prints.

1. press /   for Menu
2. press P   for Print
3. press P   for Printer
4. press R   for Range
5. press F3   all names are displayed.
6. type the name of one you want, Enter
7. Enter   to see range indicated by name
8. Enter   for Print menu
9. press G   for Go
10. press Q   for Quit

To set the line counter to top of page
Use this command when the paper is at the top of a new
sheet in the printer. The object is to synchronize the
thinking of Lotus with the actual printer paper location.

1. press /   for Menu
2. press P   for Print
3. press P   for Printer
4. press A   for Align

To clear print settings
To clear the settings to get ready to set something else do
this command.

1. press /   for Menu
2. press P   for Print
3. press P   for Printer
4. press C   for Clear

5. choose what to clear from All, Ranges, Borders, Image, Format or Device

To put a print job on Hold (3.1)

Sometimes you may want to halt the printer to load paper or do something else on the computer.

1. press /   for Menu
2. press P   for Print
3. press P   for Printer
4. press H   for Hold

To take print job off of Hold (3.1)

1. press /   for Menu
2. press P   for Print
3. press P   for Printer
4. press G   for Go

To print a graph image in (3.1)

This option cannot be done except for version 3.1.

1. press /   for Menu
2. press P   for Print
3. press P   for Printer
4. press I   for Image (graph)
5. press C   for Current (or Named)
   Optional - to format the graph:
6. press O   for Options
7. press A   for Advanced

8. press I   for Image
9. choose formats

To advance printer by one line
There are ways you can control your printer without getting up and going over to it and pressing buttons.

1. press /   for Menu
2. press P   for Print
3. press P   for Printer
4. press L   for Line

To set advanced printer options (3.1)
There are other advanced options we won't discuss. This is how you get into that area.

1. press /   for Menu
2. press P   for Print
3. press P   for Printer
4. press O   for Options
5. press A   for Advanced
6. press L   for Layout (or Fonts, etc.)
7. choose options

To print the column letters on every page
A top border is a set of rows that will print at the top of each page but below a header. Column headings are the usual.

1. press /   for Menu

2. press P   for Print
3. press P   for Printer
4. press O   for Options
5. press B   for Borders
6. press C   for Column
7. move to first row in the set
8. press .
9. move to last row of set
10. Enter

To print the row numbers on every page

A left border is a set of columns that will print at the left of each page. Usually row descriptions are set as a border.

1. press /   for Menu
2. press P   for Print
3. press P   for Printer
4. press O   for Options
5. press B   for Borders
6. press C   for Column
7. move to first row in the set
8. press .
9. move to last row of set
10. Enter

To clear the borders

This removes both borders from printing.

1. press /   for Menu
2. press P   for Print

3. press P   for Printer
4. press C   for Clear
5. press B   for Borders
6. press Q   for Quit

To name print settings (3.1)

When you change printer settings, you can save them
rather than keep resetting them.

1. press /   for Menu
2. press P   for Print
3. press P   for Printer
4. press O   for Options
5. press N   for Name
6. press C   for Create
7. type a name for the settings
8. Enter

To change named print settings (3.1)

To change or edit a print setting, recall it, change it,
rename it.

1. press /   for Menu
2. press P   for Print
3. press P   for Printer
4. press O   for Options
5. press N   for Name
6. press U   for Use
7. choose a name for the settings to modify
8. Enter

9. press /   for Menu
10. press P   for Print
11. change what you want to change

Now rename it:
12. press /   for Menu
13. press P   for Print
14. press P   for Printer
15. press O   for Options
16. press N   for Name
17. press C   for Create
18. choose the same name as in step 7
19. Enter

To delete a named print settings (3.1)
1. press /   for Menu
2. press P   for Print
3. press P   for Printer
4. press O   for Options
5. press N   for Name
6. press D   for Delete

To create a table of named print settings (3.1)
This command creates a listing of all the named print settings available. Maybe you have made more than one for different purposes. One for budgets, one for sales-type sheets, and one for general. Maybe you've made some you forgot about.

1. move to blank area to write the list.

2. press /   for Menu
3. press P   for Print
4. press P   for Printer
5. press O   for Options
6. press N   for Name
7. press T   for Table
8. Enter

To form feed to the top of next page

Another command you could do on the front panel of most printers. This is a step saver.

1. press /   for Menu
2. press P   for Print
3. press P   for Printer
4. press P   for Page

To print sample of printers capabilities (3.1)

It may be helpful to know what your printer can do when it comes to printing Lotus worksheets. Print this file and find out.

1. press /   for Menu
2. press P   for Print
3. press P   for Printer
4. press S   for Sample
5. press A   for Align
6. press G   for Go

WYSIWYG Menu commands

To select a printer to print on

If you have more than one printer in the office this is the command to switch between them. You have to switch the Lotus setting as well as the hardware from your PC to the printer. Most people use an A/B Switch box. The two printers plug into it, and the box plugs into your PC. You just turn a dial to send to the right printer.

1. press :   for Menu
2. press P   for Print
3. press C   for Configuration
4. press P   for Printer
5. press a number from 1 to 9
6. press Q   for Quit
7. press G   for Go

To print a spreadsheet

This print command or the normal one should work.

1. press :   for Menu
2. press P   for Print
3. press R   for Range (for 1st printing)
4. press S   for Set
5. move to first cell to print
6. press .
7. move to last cell to print
8. Enter
9. press G   for Go

To print in Landscape mode (sideways)

You can get more columns on a piece of paper if you turn the paper sideways. This is called landscape.

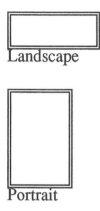

Landscape

Portrait

1. press	:	for Menu
2. press	P	for Print
3. press	C	for Configuration
4. press	O	for Orientation
5. press	L	for Landscape
6. press	Q	for Quit
7. press	G	for Go

To print to an encoded file

You can use the Print command later to print from a command line. Lotus adds extension .ENC. The purpose of this command is to make a file that can be printer in the background while you do something else ont the PC. If you don't you are waiting on Lotus until the print job is done.

1. press :   for Menu
2. press P   for Print
3. press F   for File
4. type name to call new encoded file
5. Enter

To load BPRINT for background printing

Bprint is a program that comes and installs with Lotus. To use it you must get out of Lotus and start it. Then go back into Lotus to use it.

1. press /   for Menu
2. press Q   for Quit
3. press Y   for Yes
4. type BPRINT (get to a command line if you are not)
5. Enter
6. go back into Lotus your normal way

To print in the background

To print in the background means to print a spreadsheet while you work on something else. You do not have to wait until the printing is done to do other work.

If you have not left Lotus and installed BPRINT program that comes with Lotus, do that now. See command above.

You need to print the worksheet to an encoded file as explained above if you have not done that.

1. press /   for Menu

2. press P   for Print
3. press B   for Background
4. scroll to the file name to print
5. Enter

To print to a file
1. press /   for Menu
2. press P   for Printer
3. press F   for File
4. type name of file to make
5. Enter
6. press G   for Go

WYSIWYG commands

To display or remove Wysiwyg status screen
The status screen is a screen that shows the settings of the menu you are in. Some people want to see the spreadsheet that is behind it. Usually it has the command 'press F2 to edit' at the bottom.

1. press :   for Menu
2. press P   for Print
3. press I   for Info

To change page size
You can printer letter size (8½ x 11), legal (8½ x 14), or any other size you set.

1. press :   for Menu
2. press P   for Print
3. press L   for Layout
4. press P   for Page size
5. press a number from 1 to 7 to choose

To change page size to custom dimensions
Custom is a non-standard page size.

1. press :   for Menu
2. press P   for Print
3. press L   for Layout
4. press P   for Page size
5. press C   for Custom
6. type a size for width
7. Enter
8. type a size for length
9. Enter

To change margins
1. press :   for Menu
2. press P   for Print
3. press L   for Layout
4. press M   for Margins
5. press L   for Left
6. type a number

7. Enter
8. press R   for Right (T for top, B for bottom)
9. type a number
10. Enter
11. press Q for Quit

To create a Header to appear on every page
1. press :   for Menu
2. press P   for Print
3. press L   for Layout
4. press T   for Titles
5. press H   for Header
6. type your header phrase
7. Enter
8. press Q   for Quit

To create a Footer to appear on every page
1. press :   for Menu
2. press P   for Print
3. press L   for Layout
4. press T   for Titles
5. press F   for Footer
6. type your footer phrase
7. Enter
8. press Q   for Quit

To clear a Footer
1. press :   for Menu
2. press P   for Print
3. press L   for Layout

4. press T   for Titles
5. press C   for Clear
6. press F   for Footer
7. press Q   for Quit

To clear a Header

1. press :   for Menu
2. press P   for Print
3. press L   for Layout
4. press T   for Titles
5. press C   for Clear
6. press H   for Header
7. press Q   for Quit

To create a top border

A top border is a set of rows that will print at the top of each page but below a header. Usually column headings and any underlining is set as a border.

1. press :   for Menu
2. press P   for Print
3. press L   for Layout
4. press B   for Borders
5. press T   for Top
6. move to first row in the set
7. press .
8. move to last row of set
9. Enter

To create a left border

A left border is a set of columns that will print at the left of each page. Usually row descriptions are set as a border.

1. press :   for Menu
2. press P   for Print
3. press L   for Layout
4. press B   for Borders
5. press L   for Left
6. move to first column in the set
7. press .
8. move to last column of the set
9. Enter

To clear the top border

This removes the border from printing.

1. press :   for Menu
2. press P   for Print
3. press L   for Layout
4. press B   for Borders
5. press C   for Clear
6. press T   for Top
7. press Q   for Quit

To clear the left border

1. press :   for Menu
2. press P   for Print
3. press L   for Layout
4. press B   for Borders

5. press C   for Clear
6. press L   for Left
7. press Q   for Quit

To clear all the borders
1. press :   for Menu
2. press P   for Print
3. press L   for Layout
4. press B   for Borders
5. press C   for Clear
6. press A   for All
7. press Q   for Quit

To preview how a spreadsheet will print
With all of the formatting options these days it is nice to take a look at our creations before we spend the time and paper to print them. This is how.

1. press :   for Menu
2. press P   for Print
3. press P   for Preview
4. press any key for the next page
5. press ESC when done

To set a print range
This command tells Lotus what area, or cells, you want printed. You must do this before printing.

1. press :   for Menu
2. press P   for Print
3. press R   for Range
4. press S   for Set
5. move to first cell to print
6. press .
7. move to last cell to print
8. Enter

To compress the size of print
Compression is used to reduce the size of print and graphs so more data will fit on a sheet of paper.

1. press :   for Menu
2. press P   for Print
3. press L   for Layout
4. press C   for Compression
5. press M   for Manual
6. type the % reduction (like 75)
7. Enter

To update the Default layout with yours
This command saves your newly created print Layout and tells Lotus to use it from now on.

1. press :   for Menu

2. press P   for Print
3. press L   for Layout
4. press D   for Default
5. press U   for Update

To reset the Default layout

This command replaces your Layout you made with the
original one that came with Lotus.

1. press :   for Menu
2. press P   for Print
3. press L   for Layout
4. press D   for Default
5. press R   for Restore

To start printing from a specific page

For some reason you may only want part of your
spreadsheet printed, you can do that with this command.

1. press :   for Menu
2. press P   for Print
3. press S   for Settings
4. press B   for Begin
5. type page number to start with
6. Enter

To end printing from a specific page

1. press :   for Menu
2. press P   for Print
3. press S   for Settings

4. press E   for End
5. type page number to start with
6. Enter

To assign a page number to start a range

This assigns a number other than 1 to the first page of a print job.

1. press :   for Menu
2. press P   for Print
3. press S   for Settings
4. press S   for Start-number
5. type page number to start with
6. Enter

To print more than one copy

It is faster to print multiple copies through the command than resend the whole job again.

1. press :   for Menu
2. press P   for Print
3. press S   for Settings
4. press C   for Copies
5. type the quantity
6. Enter

To print grid lines

You can print the grid lines with the sheet with this command. The default is not to. Setting the grid on the screen does not mean it will print.

1. press :   for Menu
2. press P   for Print
3. press S   for Settings
4. press G   for Grid
5. press Y   for Yes

To print the spreadsheet frame

The frame is the set of row numbers and column letters that tells you where you are on a spreadsheet.

1. press :   for Menu
2. press P   for Print
3. press S   for Settings
4. press F   for Frame
5. press Y   for Yes (default is No)

To reset WYSIWYG to default print settings

To reset Lotus from your print settings back to the default use this command.

1. press :   for Menu
2. press P   for Print
3. press S   for Settings
4. press R   for Reset

To specify a specific printer bin

Some printers come with more than one tray or shoot. This command tells Lotus which one to pull paper from.

1. press :   for Menu
2. press P   for Printer
3. press C   for Configuration
4. press B   for Bin
5. press U   for Upper Bin (L for Lower)
6. press Q   for Quit
7. press G   for Go

To specify a specific font cartridge

Some printers come with a slot that will hold a cartridge you can buy. These cartridges hold more fonts (type sizes & styles) than came with the printer. You have to tell Lotus you have them.

1. press :   for Menu
2. press P   for Printer
3. press C   for Configuration
4. press 1   for cartridge 1 (2 for second)
5. press Q   for Quit
6. press G   for Go

	B	C	D	E	F
1 BUDGET					
2					
3 ITEM	CODE	SPENT	BUDGETED	DIFF	% OVER
4 Pens	101	58.95	75.00	16.05	21.4%
5 Pencils	102	142.33	125.00	-17.33	-13.9%
6 Paper	103	195.00	250.00	55.00	22.0%
7 Misc	104	280.00	300.00	20.00	6.7%
8 Salaries	105	5432.11	5000.00	-432.11	-8.6%
9 Rent	106	950.00	950.00	0.00	0.0%
10 Utilities	107	1456.23	1500.00	43.77	2.9%
11				0.00	0.0%
12				0.00	0.0%
13					
14					

Figure 2 Working with Grid on

Chapter 7 Files

Some keyboards have an Enter key, some have a Return key. They mean the same thing.

To retrieve a file
Once you make a file you need to know how to get back up on the screen any time you want to work on it.

1. press /   for Menu
2. press F   for File
3. press R   for Retrieve
4. type name of file
   or
4. use right arrow to scroll file list
5. Enter

To save a file
You should save your work with this command every 5-15 minutes depending on how fast you work. It doesn't take much time and it is well worth the effort. I hear of so many people losing their work when it is not necessary.

1. press /
2. press F   for File
3. press S   for Save
4. type name of file
5. Enter

To change to another Directory

A directory is a container for files, or file category. You can organize what you create by putting them into different directories like the different drawers in a file cabinet. You have to make a directory at the command line, not in Lotus.

1. press /   for Menu
2. press F   for File
3. press D   for Directory
4. type new directory
5. Enter

To make a directory

You can make as many directories as you want.

1. press /   for Menu
2. press S   for System
3. type MD   for Make Directory
4. press Spacebar
5. type the name of the directory you want (8 characters)
6. Enter
7. type Exit   for returning to Lotus
8. Enter

To change directories

1. press /   for Menu
2. press F   for File
3. press D   for Directory
4. type a new disk and directory name
5. Enter

To delete a file
1. press /   for Menu
2. press F   for File
3. press E   for Erase
4. press W   for Worksheet (or Print,Graph,Other)
5. type the name of the file (or scroll to it)
6. Enter
7. press Y   for Yes to erase

To save file under a different name
Any sheet that is real important I suggest you save it under more than one name, and some of those be on floppy disk. You cannot be too safe. Disaster happens fast.

1. press /   for Menu
2. press F   for File
3. press S   for Save
4. type new name
5. Enter

To save to a floppy disk
1. press /   for Menu
2. press F   for File
3. press S   for Save
4. backspace to erase the disk and directory name
5. type A:\   (or B:\ for drive B)
6. type the name of your file
7. Enter

123

To display a full list of files
This list command won't let you retrieve or do anything
with the files here. It just shows them to you.

1. press /   for Menu
2. press F   for File
3. press L   for List
4. press W   for Worksheet (or other)
5. move to file name to retrieve
6. Enter

To update data from other spreadsheets
This command updates linked data and/or formulas that
depend on other spreadsheets.

1. press /   for Menu
2. press F   for File
3. press A   for Admin
4. press L   for Link-refresh

To enter a table of files into sheet
This command writes a list of files into a spreadsheet. You
pick from Worksheet, Graph, Print, or Other files and you
tell Lotus where to put them.

1. press /   for Menu
2. press F   for File
3. press A   for Admin
4. press T   for Table
5. press W   for Worksheets (or Graph,Print,Other)
6. Enter

7. move to first cell in upper left range to write the table
8. Enter

To copy formulas or text from another file
This command brings in formulas or text. These formulas will try to execute in the new spreadsheet. If data is not located in the cells where it expects to find them, it will ERR.

1. press /   for Menu
2. press F   for File
3. press C   for Combine
4. press C   for Copy
5. press N   for Named-range
6. type name of range to bring in
7. Enter
8. type name of file (or scroll & choose)
9. Enter

To copy values from another file
This command will bring in the value which is the answer to the formula in the original spreadsheet. It does not copy the formula itself, nor does it copy text.

1. press /   for Menu
2. press F   for File
3. press C   for Combine
4. press A   for Add
5. press N   for Named-range
6. type name of range to bring in
7. Enter

8. type name of file (or scroll & choose)
9. Enter

To import an ASCII file
An ASCII file is one with generic text. The words are not formatted in any way by a program like WordPerfect or Lotus. These files can be looked into and the text read from the DOS command line. Quite often this is the type of file exported from other programs to be taken into Lotus.

1. press /   for Menu
2. press F   for File
3. press I   for Import
4. press T   for Text (or N for Numbers)
5. choose file
6. Enter

To list files
1. press /   for Menu
2. press F   for File
3. press L   for List
4. press W   for Worksheets (or other type)
5. Enter to Enter to worksheet

To save a file with a password
Be sure to write down or remember your password. There is no way to find it in Lotus later.

1. press /   for Menu
2. press F   for File

3. press S   for Save
4. type name of file
5. press Spacebar
6. type   P   for Password
7. Enter
8. type a password up to 15 characters (no spaces)
9. Enter
10. type the password again (to verify spelling)
11. Enter

To save part of a spreadsheet
You might want to save part of a spreadsheet that will be the beginning stages of a new sheet.

1. press /   for Menu
2. press F   for File
3. press X   for Xtract
4. press F   for Formulas (or V for Values)
5. type a new file name
6. move to beginning of range to save
7. press .
8. move to end of range to save
9. Enter

	ITEM	CODE	SPENT	BUDGETED	DIFF	% OVER
	BUDGET					
	ITEM	CODE	SPENT	BUDGETED	DIFF	% OVER
	Pens	101	58.95	75.00	16.05	21.4%
	Pencils	102	142.33	125.00	−17.33	−13.9%
	Paper	103	195.00	250.00	55.00	22.0%
	Misc	104	280.00	300.00	20.00	6.7%
	Salaries	105	5432.11	5000.00	−432.11	−8.6%
	Rent	106	950.00	950.00	0.00	0.0%
	Utilities	107	1456.23	1500.00	43.77	2.9%
					0.00	0.0%
					0.00	0.0%

Figure 3 Wysiwyg zoom of 125% display

	ITEM	CODE	SPENT	BUDGETED	DIFF	% OVER
	BUDGET					
	ITEM	CODE	SPENT	BUDGETED	DIFF	% OVER
	Pens	101	58.95	75.00	16.05	21.4%
	Pencils	102	142.33	125.00	−17.33	−13.9%
	Paper	103	195.00	250.00	55.00	22.0%
	Misc	104	280.00	300.00	20.00	6.7%
	Salaries	105	5432.11	5000.00	−432.11	−8.6%
	Rent	106	950.00	950.00	0.00	0.0%
	Utilities	107	1456.23	1500.00	43.77	2.9%
					0.00	0.0%
					0.00	0.0%
	Totals		$8,514.62	$8,200.00	($314.62)	−3.84%
	Avg		1216.37	1171.43	−44.95	4.35%
	Count		7			

Figure 4 Normal size row display

Chapter 8 Graphs

To create a graph

A graph is a picture representation of some numbers and what they are.

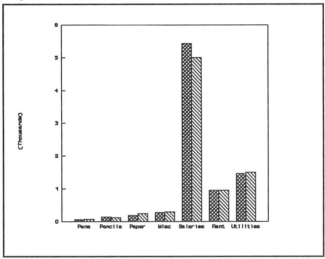

Figure 2 A sample graph

1. press /   for Menu
2. press G   for Graph
3. press T   for Type
4. press B   for Bar (or whatever kind you want)
5. press A   for 1st range to set (or other letter)
6. move to first cell of range
7. press .
8. move to last cell of range, Enter
9. press X   for X-axis (label descriptions)

129

10. move to first cell of range
11. press .
12. move to last cell of range, Enter
13. press V   for View
14. press any key when done viewing

To create legends

A legend is a guide for which piece of the graph represents what. Maybe it is to tell the years apart that were plotted, sales regions, or spent vs. budget.

1. press /   for Menu
2. press G   for Graph
3. press O   for Options
4. press L   for Legends
5. press A   for A-Range
6. type a name for A-Range, Enter
7. press L   for Legend again
8. press B   for second range
9. type the name for B-Range, Enter
10. continue to select and name ranges until done

To create a graph title

This is just what it sounds, a phrase that makes up the title for the graph.

1. press /   for Menu
2. press G   for Graph
3. press O   for Options
4. press T   for Titles
5. press F   for First line

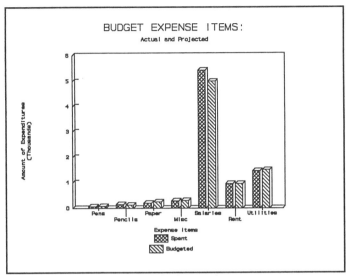

Figure 3 A graph with legends

6. type the title for top of graph, Enter
7. press S   for Second line
8. type the title for second line of title
9. Enter

To add titles to axes

If one range is the names of salesmen and one range is their sales figures you might want to make two titles to tell the viewer of the graph that is what these areas represent.

1. press /   for Menu
2. press G   for Graph
3. press O   for Options
4. press T   for Titles

5. press X   for X-axes
6. type the title for X-axes, Enter
7. press T   for Titles
8. press Y   for Y-axes
9. type the title for Y-axes, Enter
10. press QQ   for Quit

To change the axes

The program generates an unbiased scale to show the graph. Consider it carefully if you want to change the scaling. You might distort the facts by the appearance of the new graph. The numbers would be right, but the picture relationship might not be.

1. press /   for Menu
2. press G   for Graph
3. press O   for Options
4. press S   for Scale
5. press Y   for Y-Scale
6. press M   for Manual
7. press U   for Upper limits
8. type the number for highest range, Enter

To format axes

You can change whether the area under a line graph fills
or not, whether symbols are shown at the data point, both
or neither. These things can be changed for each data area
as well.

1. press /   for Menu
2. press G   for Graph
3. press O   for Options
4. press F   for Format
5. press G   for Graph
6. choose the area to format
(Lines,Symbols,Both,Neither,Area)
7. press Q   for Quit
8. press Q   for Quit

To add a background grid to graphs
A grid in the background could show you better how your bar or line graph data compare.

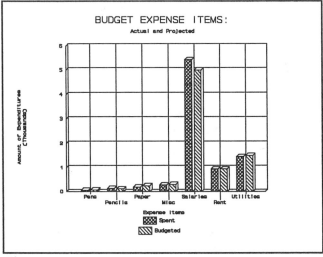

Figure 4 A graph with a grid

1. press /   for Menu
2. press G   for Graph
3. press O   for Options
4. press G   for Grid
5. press B   for Both
6. press ESC   to get back 1 menu
7. press V   for View (shows you grid & graph)

To name a graph
You can make more than one graph for each data range and not have to keep editing the graph types to see your

information plotted different ways. Once you name them
you could also save them.

1. press /   for Menu
2. press G   for Graph
3. press N   for Name
4. press C   for Create
5. type a name for the graph
6. Enter

To save the graph
1. press /   for Menu
2. press G   for Graph
3. press S   for Save
4. type a name for the File (8 char, no spaces)
5. Enter

To save other graph styles, save Spreadsheet
1. press /   for Menu
2. press G   for Graph
3. press T   for type
4. press B   for Bar (etc.)
5. press N   for Name
6. press C   for Create
7. type Name for Graph, Enter
8. press S   for Save
9. type Name for Graph, Enter

To use named graphs
Once you name graphs this command is used to retrieve them and use them.

1. press /   for Menu
2. press G   for Graph
3. press N   for Name
4. press U   for Use
5. move cursor to highlight choice, Enter
6. press Any key to Enter to menu
7. press Q   for Quit

To save graph with file
Do regular save command to save file, graph will save too.

To set a graph group
A graph group is when the x range and A through F ranges are all right next to each other. You can tell Lotus one big range and it assigns the proper letters to each column starting with the first one in the range. It saves time.

1. press /   for Menu
2. press G   for Graph
3. press G   for Group
4. move to first cell of range
5. press .
6. move to last cell of range
7. Enter
8. press C for Column-wise (or R for Row-wise)

To print a graph

You can start Lotus two ways. The first way, 123, takes you straight into the worksheet. The second way, Lotus, takes you into a main menu that has more options that using a worksheet. This command assumes you started Lotus with the command: Lotus

1. press /   for Menu
2. press Q   for Quit
3. press Y   for Yes
4. press G   for Graph from main menu
5. press I   for Image-select
6. select settings and ranges wanted (they will vary)
7. press G   for GO after selecting files

To reset a graph's settings

This command resets a graph setting so you can create a new one or change data ranges.

1. press /   for Menu
2. press G   for Graph
3. press R   for Reset
4. choose what to reset (Graph, ranges, etc)

To view a graph

1. press /   for Menu
2. press G   for Graph
3. press V   for View (F10 once graph is set once)

To make 3-Dimensional
1. press   /   for Menu
2. press   G   for Graph
3. press   F2   for Settings
4. press   3   for 3-D
5. Enter twice

To fill the area under a line graph
1. press   /   for Menu
2. press   G   for Graph
3. press   O   for Options
4. press   F   for Format
5. press   G   for Graph
6. press   A   for Area
7. press   QQ   for Quit

To choose a graph type
There are different kinds of graphs. You can ask for
whichever one you want from Bar, Pie, Line, XY, HLCO,
Stacked Bar, and Mixed.

1. press/   for Menu
2. press   G   for Graph
3. press   T   for Type
4. choose the type you want

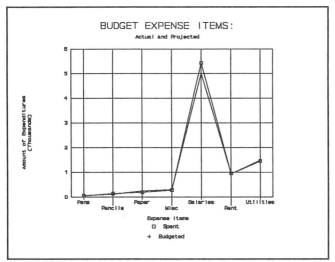

Figure 5 A line graph

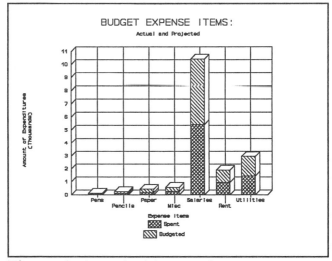

Figure 6 A stacked bar graph

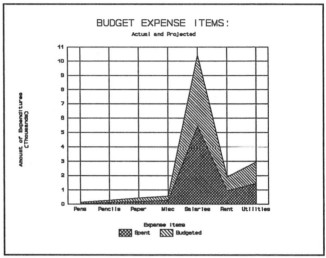

Figure 7 An area graph

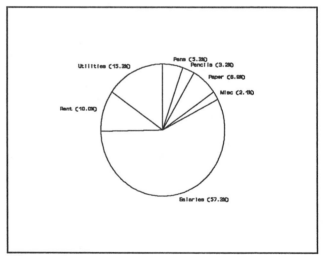

Figure 8 A pie graph

WYSIWYG *Menu commands*

To add a graph to a spreadsheet - embed it

You can put a graph into a spreadsheet. Now when you print the sheet the graph prints with it. The graph will also change each time you change a number that is in the range of data for the graph. It will automatically update.

		105	5432.11	5000.00	−432.11	−8.6%
9	Rent	106	950.00	950.00	0.00	0.0%
10	Utilities	107	1456.23	1500.00	43.77	2.9%
11					0.00	0.0%
12					0.00	0.0%
13						
14	Totals		$9,488.34	$8,200.00	($1,288.34)	−15.71%
15	Avg		1355.48	1171.43	−184.05	−119.87%
16	Count		7			

1. press :   for Menu
2. press G   for Graph
3. press A   for Add
4. press C   for Current (rather than one on disk)
5. move to beginning of range
6. press .
7. move to end of range
8. Enter

To update graphs in all active (open) files (3.1)
If you have more than one file open this command updates all of them.

1. press :   for Menu
2. press G   for Graph
3. press C   for Compute

To edit a graph
This command is to edit a graph that is embedded into the worksheet. You have to have a way to get to it.

1. press :   for Menu
2. press G   for Graph
3. press E   for Edit
4. press F3   for list of graphs
5. scroll to the one wanted on the list
6. Enter
7. choose the kind of edit to perform
8. edit the graph
9. press Q   for Quit

To jump to a specific graph
If there is more than one graph in your sheet, you may like the speed of jumping to the one of your choice.

1. press :   for Menu
2. press G   for Graph
3. press G   for Goto

4. type name of graph (or scroll to it)
5. Enter

To move a graph
You can move a graph that was inserted just like you can move a range of cells.

1. press :   for Menu
2. press G   for Graph
3. press M   for Move
4. press F3   for list of graphs
5. scroll to one wanted on list
6. Enter
7. move to new upper left corner
8. Enter
9. press Q   for Quit

To delete a graph from the worksheet
If you no longer want a graph embedded in the worksheet use this command to remove it.

1. press :   for Menu
2. press G   for Graph
3. press R   for Remove
4. press F3   for list of graphs
5. scroll to one wanted to delete
6. Enter
7. press Q   for Quit

To view a saved graph
Viewing a saved graph is different from viewing one you have made and is available just by having your spreadsheet open.

1. press :   for Menu
2. press G   for Graph
3. press V   for View
4. press P   for Pic file (or M for CGM files)
5. highlight the graph file from the list
6. Enter
7. ESC when done viewing

To display an embedded graph on full screen
Sometimes you want a better view of an embedded graph. To see the graph on the entire screen use this command.

1. press :   for Menu
2. press G   for Graph
3. press Z   for Zoom
4. press F3   for list of graphs
5. scroll to one wanted
6. Enter
7. ESC when done
8. press Q   for Quit

To display graph in color
1. press /   for Menu
2. press G   for Graph
3. press O   for Options
4. press C   for Color

5. press QQ   for Quit

To label graph data
1. press /   for Menu
2. press G   for Graph
3. press O   for Options
4. press A   for Range A
5. define range
6. Enter
7. press L   for Left of point (or other)
8. press Q   for Quit

	B	C	D	E
1	BUDGET			
2				
3	ITEM	CODE	SPENT	BUDGETED	DIFF
4	Pens	101	58.95	75.00	16.05
5	Pencils	102	142.33	125.00	−17.33
6	Paper	103	195.00	250.00	55.00
7	Misc	104	280.00	300.00	20.00
8	Salaries	105	5432.11	5000.00	−432.11
9	Rent	106	950.00	950.00	0.00
10	Utilities	107	1456.23	1500.00	43.77
11					0.00
					0.00

Figure 13 Wysiwyg zoom of 150% display

Chapter 9 Wysiwyg

WYSIWYG is an optional add-in program that lets you do more commands and formatting in Lotus. You can attach it for use once in a while, all the time, or not at all. It's main use is in formatting and appearance.

The commands available on the WYSIWYG menu are separated into the appropriate chapters by subject in this book. They are located at the end of each chapter after the standard commands. The WYSIWYG commands for formatting will be in Chapter 5 on Formatting, and so on.

To attach WYSIWYG

(What You See Is What You Get)
This is an add-in feature of Lotus. You can see and work in a graphical environment, more like Excel.

1. press /   for Menu
2. press A   for add-in
3. press A   for attach
4. scroll to WYSIWYG
5. Enter
6. press 8   to set F8 hotkey (or N,9,10)
7. press Q   for Quit

To use the menu that comes with WYSIWYG, press the colon (:) the same way you use the slash (/) to get the main menu.

You can get background grid now as well as draw lines, embed graphs into the spreadsheet, shade cells, and more.

To Detach WYSIWYG

To detach it means to remove it from memory so it is not active right now. It is still close by and able to be re-added any time you want.

1. press /   for Menu
2. press A   for add-in
3. press D   for detach
4. scroll to WYSIWYG
5. Enter

To copy WYSIWYG formats

The formatting of WYSIWYG can be copied just as easily as data in cells. It saves you from reformatting large or complex areas.

1. press :   for Menu
2. press S   for Special
3. press C   for Copy
4. move to first cell of formats
5. press .
6. move to last cell of formats
7. Enter
8. move to first cell to copy to
9. press .
10. move to last cell to copy to
11. Enter

To save WYSIWYG formats to file (export)
If you save these formats, you can retrieve them later into other files and not have to reset them.

1. press :   for Menu
2. press S   for Special
3. press E   for Export
4. type file name to create
5. Enter

To import a WYSIWYG file format
This means to use a format that you saved at some earlier time.

1. press :   for Menu
2. press S   for Special
3. press I   for Import
4. press A   for All
5. type file name to import
6. Enter

To move WYSIWYG format to other cells
The group of cells from which you moved the format returns to the default format.

1. press :   for Menu
2. press S   for Special
3. press M   for Move
4. move to first cell of formats
5. press .
6. move to last cell of formats

7. Enter
8. move to first cell to move to
9. press .
10. move to last cell to move to
11. Enter

Chapter 10 Database

The database inside lotus 1-2-3

To build a database, enter information into your spreadsheet just as you did before. The only difference is the power of the commands you now have available. You now have DATA commands.

In a database, the numbers and letters no longer function as columns and rows, they are records and fields. Each row is a record (all the stuff about a person, etc.). Any one part of the record (like person's first name) is a field.

Example: Phone Book

Record = each line (person).
Fields = First name, Last name, Address, Phone #
Think of spreadsheet this way now.

How to sort the database

Save your file first! Sorting a range of rows takes a lot of memory. I have heard a lot of wild stories from clients whose computers locked up or otherwise went nuts when they ran out of memory during a large sort. Also be sure to mark the entire row of data or Lotus will separate certain column entries from others. This is a Danger!! It can wreck your spreadsheet if separating them is not what you wanted.

1. press /   for Menu
2. press D   for Data
3. press S   for Sort
4. press D   for Data-Range
5. move to first cell of range
6. type .
7. move to last cell of range
8. Enter (highlight whole row)
9. press P   for Primary-Key
10. move to column to sort on
11. Enter
12. press A   for Ascending (D for descending)
13. Enter
14. press S   for secondary-key if desired, col #
15. press G   for GO, sort happens

How to place sequence numbers

A Data Fill is another name for sequence numbers. These numbers start with a certain number and increment by some quantity you tell it. You could start a monthly listing of invoice numbers by doing this command. You would answer the questions which number to start with, how many to add to it to get the next number, and what number to stop with. You can even increment dates this way. Type in the first date, which gives a large serial number. Then do a Fill command. Then format the whole range for dates.

1. press /
2. press D   for Data
3. press F   for Fill

4. move to beginning of range
5. type   .
6. move to end of range, Enter
7. type the # to start, Enter
8. type the # to increase each number by
9. type the sequence # to stop with

Database definitions
INPUT RANGE - a specified range of cells to query or search through. You specify the data base and the column headings that are referred to as field names.

FIELD NAMES - column headings

CRITERION RANGE - consists of field names and data. It is what Lotus uses to determine what to select.

OUTPUT RANGE - is where Lotus will put the results of the search. It must have the names of the fields you want copied forth in the topmost row.

All three ranges must have the Field Names the same and in the first row.

During a Query, Lotus Criterion range to find out what to get. Then goes to Input range to find matching records. Third, it takes the answer and displays it in the output range.

Query commands

1. FIND - highlights records retrieved one at a time.
2. EXTRACT - makes a copy of records asked for and puts them in output range.
3. UNIQUE - won't put duplicates in the output range.
4. DELETE - erases records that match from data base and deletes empty rows.
5. RESET - erases ranges and last query from memory.

To query information from the data base

The Query command is powerful. It lets you ask the spreadsheet questions and Lotus will write the answer for you into your sheet. Which invoices were for a certain sale type. Show me the ones over $1,000 and so forth.

1. Copy field names twice. One copy will be to enter the criterion range (what to search for). And the other copy is for the output range.
2. set the ranges as described below
3. type what to search for in the proper column in the criteria range.
4. press F7 to execute search

To set the query ranges

Before you can query, you need to set an input range that defines the data cells to search, an output range of where to write the answer, and a criteria range where to write the search.

1. press /   for Menu
2. press D   for Data

3. press Q   for Query
4. press I   for Input
5. move to first cell of data to search
6. press .
7. move to last cell of data range to search
8. Enter
9. press C   for Criteria
10. move to first cell of criteria column headings
11. press .
12. move to last cell of criteria column headings then
        down one row (highlighting 2 rows)
13. Enter
14. press O   for Output
15. move to first cell of output column headings
16. press .
17. move to last cell of output column headings (1 row)
18. Enter

To query
19. press E   for Extract
20. press Q   for Quit

Whole database gets copied to Output Range unless you
have already defined criteria.

Then

To select database information (query)
1. have ranges defined
2. move to Criterion range
3. type match of data you want (like what city, last name, amount greater than certain figure, etc.).
4. press F7   for Extract

Example 1:
This search will find all entries with a gross more than 2,000.

Name	Gross	SocSec	WH	Net
	>2000			

Example 2:
This search will find all records with the name Smith.

Name	Gross	SocSec	WH	Net
Smith				

Example 3:
This search will find all records with the name that begins with Sm.

Name	Gross	SocSec	WH	Net
Sm*				

Example 4:
This search will find all records with the net greater than or equal to 1000.

Name	Gross	SocSec	WH	Net
				>=1000

Example 5:
This search will find all records with the net less than 1000.

Name	Gross	SocSec	WH	Net
				<1000

Example 6:
This search will find all records with the net less than 1000, or greater than 2000.

Name	Gross	SocSec	WH	Net
				+C5<1000#or#C5>2000

• Notice that for more than one search requirement, you have to start the search criteria with a plus and make a formula, rather than an apostrophe. Lotus also requires you to put the first cell location in the column of what you are searching for.

Example 7:
This search will find all records with the net less than 2000, and greater than 1000. In other words, it finds all records within a range, from 1000 to 2000. Both conditions must be met before the record is copied to the output range.

Name	Gross	SocSec	WH	Net
				+C5>=1000#and#C5<=2000

Example 8:
This search will find all records with the net less than 2000, and greater than 1000, AND also whose name begins with an "R".

Name	Gross	SocSec	WH	Net
R*				+C5>=1000#and#C5<=2000

Query shortcut

To query without going through all the menus do the following steps. If you have queried before in this session of Lotus on this worksheet, then the ranges are still in memory, so:

1. fill in criteria to search for
2. press F7

Note 1: You can type a formula in the criterion cell also.

Note 2: You can use compound formulas using #AND# or #OR# with numbers, not labels. For labels, use 2 rows and put a label in each row.

Note 3: Do not erase criteria with the spacebar. It leaves spaces and can bring false results.

Note 2 Example:
This search will find all records with the name Smith or Jones.

Name	Gross	SocSec	WH	Net
Smith				
Jones				

To Find data
Finding data does a search and locate for the data to search for and jumps to it at it's first location in the spreadsheet.
1. define criteria and input as above
2. press /DQF   Lotus jumps to first occurrence
3. press ↓ to jump to next occurrence (keep using ↓ ↑)

To parse imported data
Parsing separates long text labels after importing a file into different cell entries. It works best with consistent data like names and addresses from a database or phone book program. These pieces of information can be broken up easily into different columns.

A format line determines how Lotus parses the label on the next row into separate columns. The types of data are: label, value, date or time. The symbols used are: D=date, L=label, S=skip, T=time, V=value, >=characters, *=space. Each group separated by one or more spaces is a block.

You would need to edit the data block if it is not wide enough to accept the length of data coming in, any data type characters Lotus defaulted to are not correct, or to remove any space that appears within a data block.

1. press /   for Menu
2. press D   for Data
3. press P   for Parse
4. press F   for Format-line
5. press C   for Create
6. press I   for Input
7. move to first cell of range (single col)
8. press .
9. move to last cell of range
10. Enter
11. press O   for Output
12. move to starting cell (upper left of range)
13. Enter
14. press G   for Go

To delete data automatically
This command deletes records from the spreadsheet that meet certain conditions.

1. press /   for Menu
2. press D   for Data
3. press Q   for Query
4. press D   for Delete

They are gone! Be careful.

To extract only unique records

Unique records are those that are not duplicates. Maybe it would be to answer which companies bought in the last 6 months. You don't need each sale transaction, only which companies, so you could choose Unique to bring out one record per company.

1. press /   for Menu
2. press D   for Data
3. press Q   for Query
4. press U   for Unique

	ITEM	CODE	SPENT	BUDGETED	DIFF	% OVER
1	ᴅᴜᴅᴳᴇᴛ					
2						
3	ITEM	CODE	SPENT	BUDGETED	DIFF	% OVER
4	Pens	101	58.95	75.00	16.05	21.4%
5	Pencils	102	142.33	125.00	−17.33	−13.9%
6	Paper	103	195.00	250.00	55.00	22.0%
7	Misc	104	280.00	300.00	20.00	6.7%
8	Salaries	105	5432.11	5000.00	−432.11	−8.6%
9	Rent	106	950.00	950.00	0.00	0.0%
10	Utilities	107	1456.23	1500.00	43.77	2.9%
11					0.00	0.0%
12					0.00	0.0%
14						
15	Totals		$8,514.62	$8,200.00	($314.62)	−3.84%

Figure 14 A Wysiwyg line box

Chapter 11 Macros

A Macro is a command that a user can make. You can record your keystrokes under a name and play them back automatically in the future whenever you need them.

Example: If you format currency with dollar signs frequently you could make a macro that did it to save you work. In the future to playback a macro, just execute the keystroke you named it under.

We will only deal with simple macros. There is a macro language you can use to make very sophisticated commands but 99% of my clients do not make anything but simple ones.

To correct simple macros, just remake them with the same name and save them over the originals.

There are two ways to create a macro
1. press ' first to start alpha mode, then type keystrokes
    to record
2. press Alt-F5 to start recording, do keystrokes, Alt-F5
    to end

To create a macro using alpha
1. move to a cell to the right of the area you will print

2. press   '   to start label mode
3. type the keystrokes that are the command(s) you want
      to have the macro do in the future (use the ~ for
      Enter)
4. Enter   when done typing them
5. press /   for Menu
6. press R   for Range
7. press N   for Name
8. press C   for Create
9. press \   for Macro Name
10. press a letter of the alphabet for the name
11. Enter twice
12. save the worksheet to save the macro

To create a macro with Alt-F5

This way to create a macro is called a keystroke recorder.
You first define a range for Lotus to write the macros for
you. Then you turn on the record feature and start doing
the keystrokes, Lotus records them all. Then you name
that range and use the macro.

1. define a learn range (see next instruction)
2. move to where you want to begin the macro
3. press Alt-F5 to begin macro recording
4. do the keystrokes you want to record
5. press Alt-F5 to end macro recording
6. move to cell that contains the macro keystrokes
7. press /   for Menu
8. press R   for Range
9. press N   for Name
10. press C   for Create

11. press \   for Macro Name
12. press a letter of the alphabet for the name
13. Enter

* Macros are always named a letter of the alphabet.

To define a Learn Range
This is the area of the sheet where Lotus will write the keystrokes you record.

1. move to beginning of range to store macros
2. press /   for Menu
3. press W   for Worksheet
4. press L   for Learn
5. press R   for Range
6. move to end of range to specify
7. Enter

To replay a macro
1. hold Alt and press letter you named macro (like: Alt-S)

To create an automatic macro
An automatic macro is one that executes immediately as soon as you open the spreadsheet. This is the only time you use a number for a macro. This is used to display user-made menus or to retrieve a certain file or anything else routine.

1. create the macro you want
2. name it \0 as described above

To create an auto loading spreadsheet
An auto loading is one that will load itself upon starting Lotus.

1. create the spreadsheet you want
2. name it AUTO123 when you save it

Macro Examples

<u>Example 1: \C</u>
To make a macro that formats dollar signs
These keystrokes will be recorded and not executed.
1. move to column to the right in a non-print area
2. press '   for the apostrophe
3. press /   for Menu
4. press R   for Range
5. press F   for Format
6. press C   for Currency
7. press 2   for 2 decimals (or 0 for none)
8. Enter
9. Enter

It looks like this: '/RFC2~

Now name it
10. press /   for Menu
11. press R   for Range
12. press N   for Name
13. press C   for Create
14. press \   for Macro name
15. press C   for Currency (made up name)
16. Enter
17. Enter   for Range (of one cell)

To execute Example 1
1. press Alt   and hold
2. hit C   do Not hold
3. release Alt

Example 2: \P
To make a macro that formats percentages
These keystrokes will be recorded and not executed.
1. move to column to the right in a non-print area
2. press '   for the apostrophe
3. press /   for Menu
4. press R   for Range
5. press F   for Format
6. press P   for Percentage
7. press 1   for 1 decimal (or 0 for none)
8. Enter
9. Enter

It looks like this: '/RFP1~

Now name it
10. press /   for Menu
11. press R   for Range
12. press N   for Name
13. press C   for Create
14. press \   for Macro name
15. press P   for Percentage (made up name)
16. Enter
17. Enter   for Range (of one cell)

To execute Example 2
1. press Alt   and hold
2. hit P   do Not hold
3. release Alt

Example 3: \D
To make a macro that formats the date
These keystrokes will be recorded and not executed.
1. move to column to the right in a non-print area
2. press '   for alpha mode
3. press /   for Menu
4. press R   for Range
5. press F   for Format
6. press D   for Date
7. press 4   for Long International
8. Enter

It looks like this: '/RFD4~

 Now name it
9. press /   for Menu
10. press R   for Range
11. press N   for Name
12. press C   for Create
13. press \   for Macro name
14. press D   for Date (made up name)
15. Enter
16. Enter   for Range

To execute Example 3
1. press Alt   and hold
2. hit D   do Not hold
3. release Alt

Example 4: \S
To make a macro that starts a sum
These keystrokes will be recorded and not executed.
1. move to column to the right in a non-print area
2. press '   for alpha
3. type @Sum(
4. Enter

It looks like this: '@Sum(

Now name it
5. press /   for Menu
6. press R   for Range
7. press N   for Name
8. press C   for Create
9. press \   for Macro name
10. press S   for Sum (made up name)
11. Enter
12. Enter   for Range

To execute Example 4
1. press Alt   and hold
2. hit S   do Not hold
3. release Alt

Example 5: \W
To make a macro that sets column width
These keystrokes will be recorded and not executed.
1. move to column to the right in a non-print area
2. press '   for the apostrophe
3. press /   for Menu
4. press W   for Worksheet
5. press C   for Column
6. press S   for Set width
7. type 15   for Width (or your choice)
8. press ~   for Enter
9. Enter

It looks like this: '/WCS15~

Now name it
10. press /   for Menu
11. press R   for Range
12. press N   for Name
13. press C   for Create
14. press \   for Macro name
15. press W   for Width
16. Enter
17. Enter   for Range

To execute Example 5
1. press Alt   and hold
2. hit W   do Not hold
3. release Alt

Suggestion:

When you set a macro range area on your spreadsheet, make 3 columns. Column one would have the name of the macro (like: \S). The second column would have the description telling what this macro does (like: format date). And the third column would have the actual macro itself you made. Be sure and skip two cells down between each macro. You need one blank cell before the next macro in a column.

To put special word commands in macros

1. be at the right spot when making the macro
2. type the appropriate word in braces

Some common special words used in macros

{down}	for down arrow
{up}	for up arrow
{left}	for left arrow
{right}	for right arrow
{pgdn}	for page down
{pgup}	for page up
{end}	for End key
{home}	for Home key
{del}	for delete
{bigright}	for ctrl-right arrow
{bigleft}	for ctrl-left arrow
{esc}	for Esc
{bs}	for backspace
{edit}	for F2
{name}	for F3

{abs}   for F4
{goto}   for F5
{window}   for F6
{query}   for F7
{table}   for F8
{calc}   for F9
{graph}   for F10
{branch}   for Goto
{menubranch} for custom menu
{quit}   for Quitting a custom menu
{?}   for Halt macro

To create a custom menu by macros

You can create your own customized menu that can contain up to 8 selections. It will appear over the worksheet just like the regular Lotus menu. Macros are behind the scenes running each option you can pick.

It depends on what commands you are going to run on the menu as to what exact steps you will do. I will outline the general creation steps first, then step you through a sample menu to make.

General steps to creating a custom menu:
1. name any ranges that need to be referred to
2. move to a clear area to the right on the worksheet
3. type {MenuBranch menu}
4. name it a macro name (like: \F   for Format menu)
5. press down arrow twice
6. type the first name of menu option to appear
7. name it the name Menu

8. press down arrow
9. type the macro commands to execute
10. press down arrow
11. type {Branch \F} (or whatever macro name)
12. move to next column and type next menu option
13. press down arrow
14. type commands to run
15. type {Branch \F}
16. move to next column and do the same

To create a format custom menu

This is a sample tutorial that walks you through the exact steps to make a menu with 4 choices on it. The first choice would be to format the cell you are on for currency. The second formats the current cell for percent. And the third choice formats the current cell for fixed 2 decimals. The last choice is quit.

1. move to a clear area to the right on the worksheet
2. type {MenuBranch menu}
3. Enter
4. press /   for Menu
5. press R   for Range
6. press N   for Name
7. press C   for Create
8. press \F   for Name of Alt-F
9. Enter
10. press down arrow twice
11. type Currency for 1st menu option
12. Enter
13. press /   for Menu

14. press R   for Range
15. press N   for Name
16. press C   for Create
17. type Menu   for Menu name
18. press down arrow
19. type Formats currency   for description
20. press down arrow
21. type '/RFC~~ for Currency commands
22. press down arrow
23. type {Branch \F} for Menubranch menu
24. move to next column beside the name CURRENCY
25. type Percents   for 2nd menu option
26. press down arrow
27. type Formats percentage   for description
28. press down arrow
29. type '/RFP~~ for Percent commands
30. press down arrow
31. type {Branch \F} for Menubranch menu
32. move to next column beside the name PERCENTS
33. type Fixed   for 3rd menu option
34. press down arrow
35. type Formats 2 decimals   for description
36. press down arrow
37. type '/RFF~~ for Fixed 2 commands
38. press down arrow
39. type {Branch \F} for Menubranch menu
40. move to next column beside the name FIXED
41. type Quit   for 4th menu option
42. press down arrow
43. type Quits this menu for description
44. press down arrow

45. type   {Quit}   for Quit command
46. Enter
47. press /   for Menu
48. press F   for File
49. press S   for Save
50. type in a name for the spreadsheet (if not named)
51. Enter (Use Alt-F to use it)

Chapter 12 Linking

To link spreadsheets

Linking spreadsheets means that numbers or formulas in one spreadsheet are tied to a second sheet. When you change anything in the first sheet, it is updated automatically in the second sheet.

There are two ways:
A) type in a formula--limited to one cell at a time
B) use the Viewer Add-in

A) To link by typing formula:
1. move to cell in receiving spreadsheet
2. type +<<
3. typc the location and name of spreadsheet to link to
4. type >>
5. type the cell to link to
6. Enter

Example: +<<Budget.wk1>>G6

B) To link by using the Viewer
1. move to correct location in receiver spreadsheet
2. Attach Viewer if not attached
3. /
4. File
5. View

6. Link
7. scroll list to file to link to
8. press right arrow key
9. move to cell(s) to link to
10. Enter if one cell only
  or
10. press period and move to show range to link to
11. Enter

The only time the files are updated is when they are retrieved and the changes read from disk. So you must retrieve each file, in order, and save it to get the change.

Example: If there were 3 sheets linked and the method was sheet one was linked to #2, and #2 was linked to #3. When you make a change in #1, you could not pull up #3 and expect to see the change. You would have to retrieve #2 first, save it, then pull up #3 and it could read the updated data from #2.

How to transfer data to another worksheet

This is copying, not really linking. Name the range in the
first spreadsheet and save it:

Be in the new spreadsheet in which to take data.
1. press /   for Menu
2. press F   for File
3. press C   for Combine
4. press A   for Add
5. press N   for Named Range
6. type   Name of range, Enter
7. choose Name of file to combine
8. Enter

9	Rent	106	950.00	950.00	0.00
10	Utilities	107	1456.23	1500.00	43.77
11					0.00
12					0.00
13					
14			———	———	———
15	Totals		$8,514.62	$8,200.00	($314.62)
16					
17	Avg		1216.37	1171.43	−44.95
18	Count		7		
19					
20					

Figure 15 A shadow box around a cell

Chapter 13 ASCII

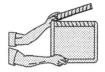

There are 255 characters & symbols represented by some keystroke on the keyboard. They can be put on the screen in almost any program by finding the number of that character and using the Alt key with the number being typed on the numbers pad.

1. look up the character you want on the chart
2. hold down the Alt key with your left hand
3. be sure num-lock key is on, in numbers pad
4. type the number on the numbers pad only
5. release the Alt key and that symbol appears

ASCII Codes

	0		1		2		3		4		5
	0	☻	1	●	2	♥	3	♦	4	♣	5
♠	6	•	7	◘	8	○	9	■	10	♂	11
♀	12	♪	13	♫	14	☼	15	►	16	◄	17
↕	18	‼	19	¶	20	§	21	▬	22	↨	23
↑	24	↓	25	→	26	←	27	∟	28	↔	29
▲	30	▼	31		32	!	33	"	34	#	35
$	36	%	37	&	38	'	39	(	40	)	41
*	42	+	43	,	44	-	45	.	46	/	47
0	48	1	49	2	50	3	51	4	52	5	53
6	54	7	55	8	56	9	57		58	;	59
<	60	=	61	>	62	?	63	@	64	A	65
B	66	C	67	D	68	E	69	F	70	G	71
H	72	I	73	J	74	K	75	L	76	M	77
N	78	O	79	P	80	Q	81	R	82	S	83
T	84	U	85	V	86	W	87	X	88	Y	89

Z	90	[	91	\	92	]	93	^	94	_	95
'	96	a	97	b	98	c	99	d	100	e	101
f	102	g	103	h	104	i	105	j	106	k	107
l	108	m	109	n	110	o	111	p	112	q	113
r	114	s	115	t	116	u	117	v	118	w	119
x	120	y	121	z	122	{	123	|	124	}	125
~	126	⌂	127	Ç	128	ü	129	é	130	â	131
ä	132	à	133	å	134	ç	135	ê	136	ë	137
è	138	ï	139	î	140	ì	141	Ä	142	Å	143
É	144	æ	145	Æ	146	ô	147	ö	148	ò	149
û	150	ù	151	ÿ	152	Ö	153	Ü	154	¢	155
£	156	¥	157	₧	158	ƒ	159	á	160	í	161
ó	162	ú	163	ñ	164	Ñ	165	ª	166	º	167
¿	168	⌐	169	¬	170	½	171	¼	172	¡	173
«	174	»	175	▒	176	▓	177	█	178	|	179
┤	180	╡	181	╢	182	╖	183	╕	184	╣	185
║	186	╗	187	╝	188	╜	189	╛	190	┐	191
└	192	┴	193	┬	194	├	195	─	196	┼	197
╞	198	╟	199	╚	200	╔	201	╩	202	╦	203
╠	204	=	205	╬	206	╧	207	╨	208	╤	209
╥	210	╙	211	╘	212	╒	213	╓	214	╫	215
╪	216	┘	217	┌	218	█	219	▄	220	█	221
█	222	▀	223	α	224	ß	225	Γ	226	π	227
Σ	228	σ	229	µ	230	τ	231	Φ	232	Θ	233
Ω	234	δ	235	∞	236	φ	237	ε	238	∩	239
≡	240	±	241	≥	242	≤	243	⌠	244	⌡	245
÷	246	≈	247	°	248	·	249	·	250	√	251
ⁿ	252	²	253	■	254		255				

There are some characters that could be very useful in creating letters or reports. Here are some of them:

Other popular symbols to use

½ 171   ¼ 172

| 179   √ 251   ¢ 155

Note: I found on some keyboards, or just with Lotus possibly, some combinations don't work, especially those over 175, or under 32. All work the same way in WordPerfect and other programs.

In these cases you would need to use the Compose command. Refer to your Lotus manual for a chart in the section on Lotus International Character Set (LICS).

To create a Compose character
1. press Alt-F1
2. type in the character representing the symbol
3. Enter

Example:
1. press Alt-F1
2. type :-
3. Enter

This produces the ÷ symbol.

* Printing ability varies with the kind and model of printer you bought. If you have any problems printing these symbols, refer to your printer manual on printing IBM characters by looking up either IBM characters or Dip switches, or contact your local computer dealer who supports you.

	ITEM	CODE	SPENT	BUDGETED	DIFF	% OVER
1	BUDGET					
2						
3	ITEM	CODE	SPENT	BUDGETED	DIFF	% OVER
4	Pens	101	58.95	75.00	16.05	21.4%
5	Pencils	102	142.33	125.00	−17.33	−13.9%
6	Paper	103	195.00	250.00	55.00	22.0%
7	Misc	104	280.00	300.00	20.00	6.7%
8	Salaries	105	5432.11	5000.00	−432.11	−8.6%
9	Rent	106	950.00	950.00	0.00	0.0%
10	Utilities	107	1456.23	1500.00	43.77	2.9%
11					0.00	0.0%
12					0.00	0.0%
13						
14						
15	Totals		$8,514.62	$8,200.00	($314.62)	−3.84%

Figure 16 Shaded totals

Chapter 14 Icons

Icons are picture symbols representing a program that can be run. The ones with Lotus come as an add-in called Icons. You must install your mouse software separately from Lotus before being able to use them. Attach the Icons add-in before using.

The first Icon palette

Icon 1 - saves the file. It is the same as / File Save

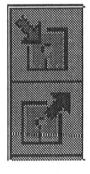

1. click on the Icon
2. type the file name (or Enter for same name)
3. Enter

Icon 2 - retrieves a file.

1. click on Icon 2
2. type the name of the file or scroll the list
3. Enter

Icon 3 - sums a range of cells. Mark a row or column and this icon will automatically sum it.

1. click & drag the mouse to mark the cell range. Include a few blank cells. The answer will be put in the last empty cell.
2. click on Icon 3

Icon 4 - charts a range. This command will automatically make a chart for the range you highlight.

1. click & drag the mouse to mark the cell range
2. click on Icon 4

Icon 5 - prints the worksheet

1. click on Icon 5

Icon 6 - previews the sheet. This command shows the file just how it will print.

1. click on Icon 6

Icon 7 - formats bold for the marked cells

1. click & drag the mouse to mark the cell range
2. click on Icon 7

Icon 8 - formats italic for the marked cells

1. click & drag the mouse to mark the cell range
2. click on Icon 8

Icon 9 - underlines the contents of cells. It does not work on empty cells. WYSIWYG

1. click & drag the mouse to mark the cell range
2. click on Icon 9

Icon 10 - enlarges the marked cells by one font size

1. click & drag the mouse to mark the cell range
2. click on Icon 10

Icon 11 - formats dollar marks for the marked cells

1. click & drag the mouse to mark the cell range
2. click on Icon 11

Icon 12 - deletes the contents of marked cells

1. click & drag the mouse to mark the cell range
2. click on Icon 12

Icon 13 - copies a range

1. click & drag the mouse to mark the cell range
2. click on Icon 13
3. click where to copy to

Icon 14 - moves a range

1. click & drag the mouse to mark the cell range
2. click on Icon 14
3. click where to move to

Icon 15 - repeats data down a column to many cells

1. click & drag the mouse to mark the cell range. Include the cell to copy and the blank cells to copy to.
2. click on Icon 15

Icon 16 - sorts the marked cells

1. click & drag the mouse to mark the cell range
2. click on Icon 16

Icon 17 - changes to the next Icon palette

1. click on Icon 17

The second Icon palette

Icon 1 - saves the file. It is the same as /
File Save

1. click on the Icon
2. type the file name (or Enter for same name)
3. Enter

Icon 2 - underlines the contents of cells. It does not work on empty cells. WYSIWYG

1. click & drag the mouse to mark the cell range
2. click on Icon 2

Icon 3 - double underlines contents of cells. It does not work on empty cells. WYSIWYG

1. click & drag the mouse to mark the cell range
2. click on Icon 3

Icon 4 - formats dollar marks for the marked cells

1. click & drag the mouse to mark the cell range
2. click on Icon 4

Icon 5 - formats commas for the marked cells

1. click & drag the mouse to mark the cell range
2. click on Icon 5

Icon 6 - formats percents for the marked cells

1. click & drag the mouse to mark the cell range
2. click on Icon 6

Icon 7 - enlarges the marked cells by one font size

1. click & drag the mouse to mark the cell range
2. click on Icon 7

Icon 8 - changes the foreground color on marked cells

1. click & drag the mouse to mark the cell range
2. click on Icon 8 until color wanted is seen
3. click on sheet anywhere to unmark

Icon 9 - changes the background color on marked cells

1. click & drag the mouse to mark the cell range
2. click on Icon 8 until color wanted is seen
3. click on sheet anywhere to unmark

Icon 10 - creates a shadow box around marked cells

1. click & drag the mouse to mark the cell range
2. click on Icon 10

Icon 11 - creates a box around marked cells

1. click & drag the mouse to mark the cell range
2. click on Icon 11

Icon 12 - creates shading around marked cells

1. click & drag the mouse to mark the cell range
2. click on Icon 12

Icon 13 - left aligns cell contents

1. click & drag the mouse to mark the cell range
2. click on Icon 13

Icon 14 - centers cell contents of marked cells

1. click & drag the mouse to mark the cell range
2. click on Icon 14

Icon 15 - right aligns cell contents of
marked cells

1. click & drag the mouse to mark the cell
range.
2. click on Icon 15

Icon 16 - centers cell contents across all
marked cells

1. click & drag the mouse to mark the cell range
2. click on Icon 16

Icon 17 - changes to the next Icon palette

1. click on Icon 17

The third Icon palette

Icon 1 - saves the file. It is the same as / File Save

1. click on the Icon
2. type the file name (or Enter for same name)
3. Enter

Icon 2 - inserts a blank row

1. move to the row above which to insert one
2. click on Icon 2

Icon 3 - inserts a blank column

1. move to the column to the right of where to insert
2. click on Icon 3

Icon 4 - deletes a row

1. move to the row to delete
2. click on Icon 4

Icon 5 - deletes a column

1. move to the column to delete
2. click on Icon 5

Icon 6 - inserts a row page break (horizontal)

1. move to the row to insert it
2. click on Icon 6

Icon 7 - inserts a column page break (vertical)

1. move to the column to insert it
2. click on Icon 7

Icon 8 - sorts the marked rows from A-Z

1. click & drag the mouse to mark the cell range
2. click on Icon 8

Icon 9 - sorts the marked rows in reverse order

1. click & drag the mouse to mark the cell range
2. click on Icon 9

Icon 10 - creates sequence number data fill

1. click & drag the mouse to mark the cell range
2. click on Icon 10
3. fill in what number to start with, Enter
4. fill in how much to increment each number, Enter
5. fill in the number to stop with, Enter

Icon 11 - recalculates the worksheet in manual mode

1. click on Icon 11

Icon 12 - inserts the current date

1. click on Icon 12

Icon 13 - draws a circle around the marked cells

1. click & drag the mouse to mark the cell range
2. click on Icon 13

Icon 14 - enlarges the cell font one size

1. click & drag the mouse to mark the cell range
2. click on Icon 14

Icon 15 - runs a macro and steps through to find errors

1. click on Icon 15

Icon 16 - runs a macro

1. click on Icon 16
2. choose macro name, Enter

Icon 17 - changes to the next Icon palette

1. click on Icon 17

The fourth Icon palette

Icon 1 - saves the file. It is the same as / File Save

1. click on the Icon
2. type the file name (or Enter for same name)
3. Enter

Icon 2 - moves left one cell

1. click on Icon 2

Icon 3 - moves right one cell

1. click on Icon 3

Icon 4 - moves up one cell

1. click on Icon 4

Icon 5 - moves down one cell

1. click on Icon 5

Icon 6 - starts Help system

1. click on Icon 6

Icon 7 - jumps cursor to Home cell A1

1. click on Icon 7

Icon 8 - jumps cursor to the end of the worksheet

1. click on Icon 8

Icon 9 - moves cursor down to first intersection of blank and non-blank cell

1. click on Icon 9

Icon 10 - moves cursor up to first intersection of blank and non-blank cell

1. click on Icon 10

Icon 11 - moves cursor right to first intersection of blank and non-blank cell

1. click on Icon 11

Icon 12 - moves cursor left to first intersection of blank and non-blank cell

1. click on Icon 12

Icon 13 - jumps cursor to a specific cell location (goto)

1. click on Icon 13

Icon 14 - finds and/or replaces text in cells

1. click & drag the mouse to mark the cell range
2. click on Icon 14
3. type words to search for, Enter
4. press L   for Labels
5. press R   for Replace (or Find)
6. type replacement words, Enter
7. press A   for All (or R for Replace one)

Icon 15 - (undo) undoes your last
command

1. click on Icon 15

Icon 16 - deletes a range

1. click & drag the mouse to mark the cell
range
2. click on Icon 16

Icon 17 - changes to the next Icon palette

1. click on Icon 17

The fifth Icon palette

Icon 1 - saves the file. It is the same as /
File Save

1. click on the Icon
2. type the file name (or Enter for same name)
3. Enter

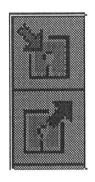

Icon 2 - retrieves a file

1. click on Icon 2
2. type file name or scroll to it
3. Enter

Icon 3 - sums a range of cells. Mark a row or column and this icon will automatically sum it.

1. click & drag the mouse to mark the cell range. Include a few blank cells. The answer will be put in the last empty cell.
2. click on Icon 3
sums a range

Icon 4 - charts a range

1. click & drag the mouse to mark the cell range
2. click on Icon 4

Icon 5 - inserts a chart into the sheet

1. click & drag to mark the range to put chart in
1. click on Icon 5

Icon 6 - edits an embedded chart

1. click on chart to edit
2. click on Icon 6

Icon 7 - edits text in a range

1. click & drag to mark the range to put chart in
2. click on Icon 7

Icon 8 - prints the spreadsheet

1. click on Icon 8

Icon 9 - previews a sheet before printing

1. click on Icon 9

Icon 10 - copies range

1. click & drag to mark the range to copy
2. click on Icon 10
3. click in the first cell where you want to put it

Icon 11 - moves a cell range

1. click & drag to mark the range to move
2. click on Icon 11
3. click in the first cell where you want to put it

Icon 12 - copies WYSIWYG formatting

1. click & drag to mark the range to copy
2. click on Icon 12
3. click & drag to mark the range to format

Icon 13 - copies a cell to other cells. This is a good quick copy down or right command.

1. click & drag to mark the range with the first cell being the thing to copy
2. click on Icon 13

Icon 14 - makes cell contents bold

1. click & drag the mouse to mark the cell range
2. click on Icon 14

Icon 15 - makes cell contents italic

1. click & drag the mouse to mark the cell range
2. click on Icon 15

Icon 16 - clears WYSIWYG formatting

1. click & drag the mouse to mark the cell range
2. click on Icon 16

Icon 17 - changes to the next Icon palette

1. click on Icon 17

The sixth Icon palette

Icon 1 - adds an icon to your custom palette. Palette number one is your palette you can customize.

1. click on the icon
2. move to the palette of your choice
3. click on the icon to add to custom palette

Icon 2 - deletes an icon from your custom palette

1. click on the icon
2. move to the custom palette
3. click on the icon to delete

Icon 3 - moves an icon to a different spot on the custom palette

1. click on the icon
2. click on the icon to move
3. click on the new spot to put it

Icon 4 - lets you define a user icon on user palette

1. click on Icon 4
2. press A   for Assign macro to icon
3. fill out the information asked for
4. Enter

The seventh Icon palette

The seventh Icon palette has user defined Icons you make
with the 4th Icon on
Palette 6.

Chapter 15 Add-ins

To auto attach an add-in

When you auto attach an add-in it means that each time you start Lotus, this add-in will load into memory without you having to do a command manually.

1. press /   for Menu
2. press W   for Worksheet
3. press G   for Global
4. press D   for Default
5. press O   for Other
6. press A   for Add-in
7. press S   for Set
8. press 3   for next number (or whatever #)
9. scroll to the add-in to set
10. Enter
11. Enter   for No hot key set
12. press Y   for Yes
13. press Q   for Quit
14. press Q   for Quit

To cancel an auto attach add-in
1. press /   for Menu
2. press W   for Worksheet
3. press G   for Global
4. press D   for Default
5. press O   for Other
6. press A   for Add-in

7. press C   for Cancel
8. press 3   for one to cancel (or whatever #)
9. press Q   for Quit
10. press Q   for Quit

To attach Backsolver

Backsolver will solve problems backwards to give you an answer, like how much house can I buy for $1200 a month?

1. press /   for Menu
2. press A   for Add-in
3. press A   for Attach
4. scroll to Backsolver, Enter
5. Enter   for No-key
6. press I   for Invoke
7. scroll to Backsolver, Enter
8. press F   for Formula-cell
9. move to cell with formula (like payment)
10. Enter
11. press V   for Value
12. type in value (like 1200)
13. Enter
14. press A   for Adjustable
15. move to adjustable cell (like principle)
16. Enter
17. press S   for Solve

The Macro Manager

A macro is a command you can make by recording keystrokes. There are advanced macros you can make using words, expressions, and conditions but most of them are simple work savers that get stored in an individual spreadsheet. The macro manager lets you make macros that can be stored in a library and recalled no matter which spreadsheet you are in.

To attach the Macro Manager
1. press /   for Menu
2. press A   for Add ins
3. press A   for Attach
4. scroll to Macro Manager
5. Enter
6. press Q   for Quit
7. Enter

To invoke the Macro Manager menu
1. press /   for Menu
2. press A   for Add ins
3. press I   for Invoke
4. scroll to Macro Manager
5. Enter

To load a particular library
1. press /   for Menu
2. press A   for Add ins
3. press I   for Invoke
4. scroll to Macro Manager
5. Enter

Add-ins

6. press L   for Load
7. scroll to one of the library names
8. Enter

The file extension for libraries is .MLB

To use Viewer to Browse files
This add-in can view the files without retrieving them.
1. press /   for Menu
2. press A   for Add-in
3. press A   for Attach
4. scroll to Viewer
5. Enter

Now to use it:
To retrieve a file using Viewer
1. press /   for Menu
2. press A   for Add-in
3. press I   for Invoke
4. scroll to Viewer
5. Enter
6. press R   for Retrieve (Browse to just view)
7. scroll list to see the one wanted
8. Enter   (to retrieve)

There is a Tutor add-in to help you learn Lotus that is not discussed in this book.

The Auditor

The Auditor is an add-in program that will help you trace down the cause of formula errors. There are 3 kinds of errors in which it can help:

1. circular reference
2. dependents - cells that refer to a cell
3. precedents - cells that affect the result

To attach the Auditor
1. press /   for Menu
2. press A   for Add-in
3. press A   for Attach
4. scroll to Auditor
5. Enter
6. press 8   for Alt-F8 hotkey (or 9 or 10)
7. press Q   for Quit

To invoke (start) Auditor menu
1. press Alt-F8   (or what key you assigned)

To set the audit mode to Trace
The trace method of reporting would have the cursor jump to each occurrence that Lotus found of whatever you are checking.

1. press Alt-F8   (or other hotkey)
2. press O   for Options

3. press T   for Trace
4. press QQ   for Quit

To trace for any circular reference errors
A circular reference is a cell with a formula that directly or indirectly somehow refers to itself.

1. press Alt-F8   (or other hotkey)
2. press C   for Circular reference
3. move to the upper left cell highlighted as source
4. Enter

Lotus highlights (or does whatever optional setting you do) each cell that is involved.

To find the cells a formula is dependent on
If you are having trouble with a formula it would make sense you might want to know what cells your formula is dependent on. This command will do that.

1. press Alt-F8   (or other hotkey)
2. press P   for Precedents
3. move to the cell to find out about
4. Enter
5. press F   for Forward search (or B for Back)
6. press F   for Forward search until beeps
7. press QQ   for Quit when done searching

To find the formulas that depend on a cell
Before you delete or change a formula you might like to check and see what cells depend on it. They would be messed up if not found.
1. press Alt-F8   (or other hotkey)
2. press D   for Dependent
3. move to the cell to find out about
4. Enter
5. press F   for Forward search (or B for Back)
6. press F   for Forward search until beeps
7. press QQ   for Quit when done searching

To find all formulas
This command would find all formulas in the spreadsheet no matter where they were and let you know what was a formula.
1. press Alt-F8   (or other hotkey)
2. press F   for Formula
3. cursor jumps to first formula
4. press F   for Forward until beeps
5. press QQ   for Quit

To attach the Icons
1. press /   for Menu
2. press A   for Add-in
3. press A   for Attach
4. scroll to Icons
5. Enter
6. press 8   for Alt-F8 hotkey (9, 10, or N)
7. press Q   for Quit

Index

/ 32
@AVG 69
@CHAR 69
@COUNT 69
@date 42, 69
@Hlookup 75
@IF 69
@SUM 69
@TODAY 69
@Vlookup 75
3-Dimensional 138
Absolute 48
Add 67, 70
Add-in 213
Advance printer 101
Advanced printer options . . . 101
Align 61
Align text across cells 64
Alignment 19
Alt-F5 164
And/Or 74
Appearance 56
Area 138
ASCII 126
ASCII Codes 181
Assign a word name 34
Attach WYSIWYG 147
Auditor 217
Auto loading 166
Automatic macro 165
Average 71
Axes 132
Background color 88
Background grid 134
Background printing 108
Backsolver 214
BASICS 17
Bin 119
Bold 87

Border 101
Box 90
BPRINT 108
Bright 57
Cancel 41
Cancel a menu 41
Cell reference formats 68
Cell-Pointer 57
Circular reference 218
Clear 25
Clear all the borders 114
Clear the borders 102
Close window 83
Color 88, 144
Colors 54
Column to widen 60
Column width 80
Combination 27
Combine 125
Commands 21
Commas 79
Compose 183
Compress 115
Convert 49
Copy 35
Correcting mistakes 72
Correction 18
Count 71
CRITERION 153
Currency 78
Custom dimensions 110
Custom menu 173
Danger 47
Data Fill 50
Database 151
Date 41
Decimals 77
Default 58
Delete 34

Delete a file 123
Delete a graph 143
Delete a range name 34
Delete a row 40
Deleting rows & columns 82
Dependent 218
Detach WYSIWYG 148
Directory 122
Display 55
Display named ranges 34
Divide 67
Dollar marks 78
DOS 43
Draw lines 89
Edit 20
Edits 32
Embed 141
Encoded file 107
Enlarge cells 58
Entering 31
Erase a range 33
Erase one cell 34
Error 20
Explanation 32
Exponent 67
EXTRACT 154
F2 32
F3 34
F5 44
F7 158
FIELD 153
Filename 25
Files 20, 121
Fill 50
Find 20, 154, 159
Fix titles 84
Floppy 123
Font 63
Font cartridge 119
Footer 97, 111
Form feed 105
Format a date 42
Formatting 77

Formula 67
Formulas 31
Frame 56
Frmt 20
Functions 67
Goto DOS 43
Graph 129
Graph group 136
Graph styles 135
Graph type 138
Graphics 55
Grid 55, 134
Header 96, 111
Headings 51
Help 20, 27
Hide columns 38
Hold 100
Horizontal & vertical titles . . . 86
Horizontal tables 75
Icons 185
If 72
Import 126
Imported data 159
Insert a blank row 39
Intensities 57
Italic 87
Jump 44, 142
Label 20, 61
Label graph data 145
Landscape 107
Layout 115
Learn 164
Left border 113
Legends 130
Library 215
Line counter 99
Lines 89
Link 177
List 26, 43
List of files 39, 124
Lock the row headings 84
Logical 68
Lookup table 75

Macro 163
Macro Examples 167
Macro Manager 215
Margins 95
Menu 20
Mistakes 72
Modes 20
Mouse 24, 28
Move a graph 143
Move a range 37
Move rows & columns 82
Moving 18, 44
Multiply 67
Name a graph 134
Name a range 33
Name print settings 103
Named-Style 93
Names 20
Negative numbers 89
Number pages 98
Numbers, ... 31
Operators 28
ORDER OF CALCULATION   73
Orientation 107
OUTPUT 153
Page 60
Page break 39
Page numbering 96
Page size 110
Page-Breaks 56
Parentheses 74
Parse 159
Password 126
Percent 79
Pic file 144
Point 20, 63
Pointing 28
Portrait 107
Precedents 218
Preview 114
Primary-Key 152
Print 26, 95, 106
Print a graph 100

Print grid lines 118
Print in the background 108
Print job on Hold 100
Print range 115
Print settings 99
Print the row numbers 102
Print the spreadsheet frame . . 118
Print to a file 109
Printer bin 119
Protecting 44
Query, ... 153
Quit 25
Range 33
Ready 20
Recalculation 45
Redisplay column 38
Relative 48
Release titles 86
Remove shading 92
Replace 26, 52
RESET 154
Reset WYSIWYG 118
Retrieve 25, 121
Row display 57
Rows 57
Rows on the screen 57
Sample of printers capabilities 105
Save 24, 121
Save the graph 135
Scroll 41
Scroll both windows together . 84
Search 52
Secondary-key 152
Select a printer 106
Sequence 50
Sequence numbers 152
Serial date 41
Shade cells 91
Shadow box 90
Sideways. 107
Signs 67
Sort 43, 151
Split the screen 83

Spreadsheets 22
Start 19
Start a new page 39
Stat 20
Status screen 109
Styles 93
Subtract 67
Sum 70
Switch 53
Synchronized scrolling 84
Table 104
Table of files 124
Text attribute 65
Text, ... 31
Title 130
Top border 112, 113
Trace 217
Transfer data 179
Transpose. 53
Type 26
Typestyle 63
Underline 92
Undo 50
Unhide columns 38
UNIQUE 154, 161
Unprotect 45
Update 58, 124
Update graphs 142
Value 21
Vertical tables 75
Vertical titles 85
View a graph 137
View a saved graph 144
Viewer 177, 216
Wait 21
Width 59
Words 26, 61
Wrap 51
WYSIWYG 147
WYSIWYG file format 149
WYSIWYG formats 148
Xtract 127
Y-Scale 132

Zero 86
/ 30